Married to
The Bad Guy

Copyright © 2019 Meagan Sparks. All rights reserved. This book or any portion thereof may not be reproduced or used in any manner whatsoever without the express written permission of the publisher except for the use of brief quotations in a book review. Printed in the United States of America

First Printing

978-1-943284-44-3 (pbk)

978-1-943284-45-0 (ebk)

A2Z Books, LLC Lithonia, GA 30058 www.A2ZBooksPublishing.net. Manufactured in the United States of America A2Z Books Publishing has allowed this work to remain exactly as the author intended, verbatim.

CONTENTS

Acknowledgments v
Preface vii
Chapter 1: The Move 1
Chapter 2: 13 & Pregnant 6
Chapter 3: She's Dead 15
Chapter 4: Welcome To ATLANTA 25
Chapter 5: The Point Of It All 35
Chapter 6: The Flip 40
Chapter 7: Free At Last 51
Chapter 8: Still Goin' In 57
Chapter 9: Paralyzed To The Streets 62
Chapter 10: Can't Raise A Man 71
Chapter 11: Last Name: Alexander 80
Chapter 12: The Indictment 86
Dedication 94
Epilogue 96

ACKNOWLEDGMENTS

Let me just say first and foremost that I want to thank God. For simply empowering me with the strength, ambition, dedication, and courage to take on each and every last one of the dreams and aspirations I've had and will have in this lifetime. I've taken what you've placed in me for granted many times. Thinking this is just how we are. Not realizing that there are so many others who could only wish and hope to ever believe in themselves enough to trust your promises and to do what they want to do. So many die without ever living. Grow old and look back at a bunch of "I should have's."

I'm fearless because of you! When you're ready for me to come home, I'll have had lived a full life because whatever purposes there are that *you* have planned for me, I'll have done. I don't have to be this super deep, Bible-toting woman for you to continue to work through me and in my favor; my love for you is endless. I want to thank my Mom, Diane McKinney, for being a rider. For being a risk taker for your kids and planting in me the spirit of wanting the best and settling for nothing less than.

My OG, I love you! My GiGi, the one and only LeeEsther Moore for raising me to be a woman of high quality. Without you, I'm not much, and I think you know that. My nephews Kae'lehn & Kae'meron Dotson for being my WHY. The only people in this world I feel like I have something to prove to. You two are amazing and are WHY I would never let up. My sister, Tiffany Vaughn. You're a beautiful person. I'm ready when you are. My cousin April James, Julia, Bridgette Cook, LaToya Brewer for being real friends. CleAira Anderson, the most loyal living being I've met in my life.

You taught me what that word meant. I trust you with my house, purse and around my man. Your children should be honored to have you as a Mother; you remind me of mine – that says a lot. Ronne Brown for helping me on a GirlCEO journey that changed my life, being a great mentor and always being there to pour into and motivate me. My Publisher, Synovia Dover-Harris and the entire team at A2Z Books, thank you for your patience with this project. I'm a lot to deal with, and you've never made me feel like it.

Lastly, I'd like to thank *you*, for inspiring me to write. Look what you brought out of me! Wow. Thank you so much for *everything* you've done for me and my family. I appreciate you more than you would know. Not perfect, but you're a real King in my eyes. No matter where life takes us, I will always respect you for being who you've been to me since the summer of 2009. You've loved me more than you've loved yourself. They've always had to go through *you* to get to *me*. People would be surprised to know how close we really are. We roll thick as thieves' man; they better ask somebody. Nothing is coming between us but time.

I love you so much Darius,

Meagan.

PREFACE

It was life-changing for me the day I woke up to a house surrounded by unmarked cars, officers with their guns drawn... about seventeen of them. That was enough I had thought, until later that day when the headlines went up and from there, only got worse.

> LaDarius D. Alexander, 24, of the far east side, was arrested on Monday, charged with one complicity count to murder and robbery..." To, "Man gets nearly 12 years for his role in 2011 south side robbery. Alexander wasn't indicted in the 2011 case until October. At Wednesday's hearing, he also pleaded guilty to one count each of participating in a criminal gang and illegally possessing a gun in an unrelated 2014 case. McIntosh sentenced him to eight years in that case, to run concurrently with the sentence in the 2011 case.

That was what the Columbus Dispatch and 10tv news reported about my Husband. I felt robbed of my life as I knew it. In the amount of time it took them to handcuff and yell whatever it was they were saying, my entire world was turned upside down! Even though I felt the way I did, I can't say I was surprised. I was heartbroken from the look in his eyes. He knew it was over!

This is just what happens when you put your trust in the streets. They trick you off of them! By cell or casket, and you don't take your pick. For me, it wasn't *if* they were coming, it was *when*. "*They*" as in the D.A.'s with the indictments or the man behind the trigger that would have ended his life. All things eventually catch up with you either for the good or bad you've done. "Everybody gets a turn." LA always told me that and it's true.

You never really have a clear mental when you're in a relationship with a man who is living a life like this. You just don't. That's something you have to be willing to sacrifice too. They don't tell you that in the beginning, but that's what it will come to at some point. Even when everything seems like it's perfect and couldn't get better, you're still sacrificing. When he walked out of the door each day, I thought about what could happen. I lived in constant fear because you never know.

I'm writing this now with tears in my eyes and chills through my body from thinking back to what I dealt with. I honestly felt as if my days with him were numbered. Like maybe I was counting down, but I didn't know the final number. I made sure we created memories together that would last a lifetime. Even though I intentionally pulled him away from what I could see would destroy him, I knew realistically I couldn't prevent it all.

So in understanding that, I just tried my best to prepare my heart for whatever life gave me. Prepare my mind so that I would never be one to lose it. Prepared us both in case something happened, or in my mind, *when* it happened. LaDarius didn't know then, but the reason I would record him all the time and take pictures was because of that countdown I felt like I was on. If I need them, I had them. Our text messages, I would think to myself like this could be our last time speaking to each other, I'm not deleting this. Paranoid! This is the shit I was trying to prevent from happening to my family. I guess I failed. He promised me and his son he would never leave us; I guess he lied. Either that or LA failed me, but who's to judge? We'd had enough of being judged from Franklin County.

Chapter 1

THE MOVE

November 2001. My Mom had the whole house packed up when we got home from school. She had talked to us about moving to Hawaii before, but we didn't think she was serious. I was confused this day because that's where it looked like she was taking us; away. I saw Shoonie working the last of our belongings into this 2001 white Ford Windstar. It was brand new. I was trying to figure out if this was ours and where the hell she got the money from to up and move all of us out of LA, just like that.

We're moving to Ohio. I mean, we'd visited Columbus a couple of times in the summer with GiGi, and it was ok, but it was no place for some *LA girls* to call home. We're city, Columbus was country to us. Cows, streets without sidewalks, farms... a damn near different world. My Mom was a single mother. Four kids. My brother lived in East LA with his Dad, step Mom, and their family his whole life. My Mom still gave him what she gave the rest of her kids, but he didn't live with us.

His dad kidnapped him when he was a baby... long story. Tiffany's Dad helped with her growing up, and Taneisha's Dad wasn't around, like mine – whoever he's supposed to be or wherever he is. My Mom busted her ass, hustling and taking chances to raise us and did a damn good job. So yeah, that's the crew. It was me, Taneisha, Tiffany, and my Mom all packed up and ready to hit this road across the country, to Ohio. To live. Yes, she dead ass drove from 104th & Vermont in South Central to Dundee & S. Hamilton Rd. in Columbus, Ohio in a minivan with her girls in tow. Our lives squished in the trunk. She left everything else where it was. We fought, argued, laughed, cried and sang 22,000 miles. It took us five days to get there. Five!

The first time I'd ever seen seasons – winter. First time I'd ever seen real snow, squirrels, deer, the whole scene. I'd never felt temperatures so low. In my classes at the new school, I'd met a lot of other little girls who actually all ended up being my friends through High School. Tiffany adjusted more slowly to the change, as she was older than me and more attached to the friends she already had a history with. We were both sad, but I'd say because she was older, she was a lot more sad to be leaving her friends behind in Cali. Tiffany was out of control back home, called herself gang banging.

Ohio was just too slow for her. So slow that she went from gang member to a straight "A" student in school, who took piano lessons every week. Bored out of her mind. Months went by, and we started being more comfortable with our transition. Mom and Taneisha went back to California because there weren't any doctors my Mom trusted to care for Taneisha on the East Coast. She left us with GiGi for about two years then came back. We would visit Cali all the time; Grandmommy made that happen.

My Grandmommy and my auntie Michelle also raised me in their home in Carson. As a matter of fact, I spent most of my time there when I was younger. So when we left, she flew us in every school break and we stayed every summer. Living in Ohio started to not be as bad because we were still able to go home when we wanted to.

Tiffany met Kelleè at Walnut Ridge, in I think their English class. They got close quick. She started coming over to our house, and we'd go over to hers after school. Same with my friends. We all lived blocks away from each other in East Columbus. Going over to Kelleè's house was when I found Elaine Rd. or Elaine Rd. found me. I was kind of shocked to find out that it was a hood. I was used to hoods looking way worse. Projects, homeless people laying around on the grounds, living in tents, groups of crack heads smoking, liquor stores on every block.

It was nothing close to what I was used to seeing, but it was still wild and the kids out there were wild too. Every day, it was something to get into, and that's exactly what I did. All through middle school, I was in some shit. I had the most fun back then, but I also put myself in situations; bad situations that I could've avoided. I don't regret any of it though. Everything I put myself through, I learned from. Not only did I learn, I grew – more like grew up, fast. I feel that moving to Ohio was more of a better move for my Mom than it was for us. She got herself together when we moved out of LA. But for Tiffany and Me... well, we went through some shit.

I met the first guy I had ever loved or touched out there in the neighborhood and around the same people I'd met when we first moved to Ohio. He was I think maybe four years older than me, like 17. He was dark skinned, tall, very slim, with the crustiest top lip you'll ever see on someone. He had just came home from a Juvenile prison some weeks before. We were at Aunt Sandy's house; this was November 1st, 2004. The morning after Ashley's birthday party. I saw him the night before, and he stood out. From what I was seeing, it was like all the females wanted his attention and all the boys either wanted to be around or far away from him. I wouldn't say I was immediately attracted to him though; I was just paying attention.

When we met, I was laying down in the basement, and he came from out of nowhere, talking. He wouldn't shut up. He kept asking me a bunch of questions, then asked if he could lay next to me and talk. I was scared as hell and intimidated by what I'd seen at the party and what he'd said, but I liked it. What he was really trying to do was laugh me out my panties though. In the months to come, I spent damn near most of my days with SAJ. I came to Sandy's house so much, waiting on him; my cover got blown quick. They all knew it. I was skipping school, having him pick me up, sneaking him into my Mom's house, go to his house and do what we weren't supposed to do. I was glued.

So young, I hadn't even thought about my virginity being taken, so when this happened, I didn't know what to do. I didn't understand what I was feeling; I didn't know what to expect from him either. I was just taking it day to day, but getting more and more attached as time passed. For years SAJ was all I knew. There were many nights that I laid with him on the floor, in the trap, with no cover, just his big black leather Pelle Pelle coat over us keeping me warm.

Funny thing about it, I guess that was just where I wanted to be – with him wherever. At that age, he was a jack boy. It would make more sense to say he sold drugs on the side. Whatever he was doing, I was there. Some of those licks, I helped to set up. We would get ready and go together. That was how for him I was. The kind where you don't think about what you're doing, you just do it. I'm glad I'm not that girl today and was never hurt behind anything... I'll just leave it at that.

That wouldn't even cross my mind today. Back then it was never who I was as a person, to take from people? To put people and myself in dangerous situations that could've ended our lives? Hell no! But just like a lot of girls at that age, I was down for this boy who I thought was the world. I was with whatever he was with. This reason alone is why it's so important to be super involved in your kid's lives. Not as their friend, but their parent.

You never know who their friend, boyfriend, or girlfriend are influencing them to be. You have no clue how much danger they're putting themselves in just doing dumb shit, so pay attention to the things they're paying attention to and watch who you allow them to spend time with. Remember that everybody is raised differently. It's so much that can be avoided just by being more involved and understanding these young girls and boys.

My Mom was more of a provider. We didn't want for too much of anything. But the things I did need, now looking back, like those one on one talks. I'm not sure if she couldn't give it to me or she just didn't sit still for long enough to do. Either way, if she had done that with me, it would've definitely made a difference. I wouldn't have done a lot of the things I did. I won't say that I was looking for guidance from SAJ that a Father would give his daughter, but I will say that young girls who don't have male figures in their lives end up how I was.

Figuring boys out all by myself. Everything from sex, love, broken hearts and manipulation. I believe my experiences with him equipped me for every boy that came after. I found out what bullshit was at an early age, so from that point, I really didn't waste too much time with anybody's son at all. I always had a boyfriend. I was always in a relationship. I've never, still to date, jumped from one bed to the next always with another guy. I can either see myself around you for a lifetime or I homeboy and friend zone you, period. I still went through my shit though. I still struggled, only I did it when I was really young. When other girls were at sleepovers and dance practice, I was out having adult women problems.

Chapter 2

13 & PREGNANT

Seventh grade. I remember this morning like it was yesterday. I had gotten placed at iPass. An alternative school, for 30 days to avoid expulsion from Sherwood. I was there for pushing my teacher that was trying to break up a fight between another girl and me. At this school, we weren't allowed to pass notes. Well, I sat at my desk and wrote up a birth certificate. I included all the details too. The baby's expected date of birth, the Mother and Father's name, everything. The teacher called my name, *Ms. Sparks! You got somethin' over there you want to share with the class?* "N- -," he cut me off. *Sure you do, bring it here!*

Here he is thinking it's another note getting ready to be passed through his classroom. I walked it to him damn near shaking! I knew exactly what was about to happen. He read the paper for about thirty seconds and said, *come with me, Meagan. The rest of you keep quiet!* He looked so concerned; he knew I wasn't scribbling all this for nothing. We went into the Principal's office. Next thing I heard was; "*We're faxing over a copy of it now Ms. McKinney, thank you.*" I was scared as hell!

All I could think was when my Mom gets this fax she was going to be on my ass! I could imagine her face when she read what I'd written. Later that day, after school when I got home, to my surprise, my Mom didn't say anything. Everything was *normal*, so I thought. She didn't say a word about the fax, so I assumed she never got it. I was good! The next Morning was when everything got weird. My Mom woke me up early in the morning. Real early. She never did that. I was so hungry; you should've seen me! I poured three huge bowls of cereal, Rice Crispy Treats, back to back.

My Mom was right there, sitting across from me at the table, which was already strange. We *never* sat together at the kitchen table as a family and ate. She watched me stuff my face spoon full after spoon full. Eventually, she looked me in my eyes as if she just already *knew* I was about to lie and said, "*You sure are eating a lot. That's a lot of cereal. Why're you so hungry?*" "I'm not. I just didn't eat nothin' last night."

"*Yeah, ok.*" She got up and started loading the dishwasher. "*You've got to get this physical done for iPass; your doctor's appointment is at 11.*" In my mind I was thinking like, oh this bitch set me up! This is a setup! This school don't need no damn physical! She only wanted to find out for sure why I was eating the way I was, why I was so tired and why I'd be in class writing Birth Certificates. She ain't no dummy!

We got to Children's Close to Home on E. Broad St. We check in; the staff was looking weird, everything was weird. I felt like I was in a daze. My Mom and the Nurses were whispering back and forth to each other; I can't explain my level of nervousness. Every part of my body was sensitive to touch. I could've thrown up; I was that scared. You would've thought my Mom flashed a gun at me. We both went into the room and not even five minutes passed before the Nurse brought in a cup!

"*Meagan, you can go ahead and get us some urine in here so we can check your iron levels.*" I already knew what time it was after that. Only a matter of minutes before it was about to go down! I was trying to stall out on time or have them tell us to come back another day, so of course, I'll say I can't go. "*I don't have to pee.*" Everybody, at what seemed to be at once, said, "*Oh we'll wait. We've got plenty of time. Just drink some more water!*"

As terrified as I was for my Mom to find all this out, and to hear it myself from a Doctor, I went into that bathroom. I came out to see everyone standing around the Nurse's station waiting for me. Keep in mind; the office was closed for the day by then. It was so silent that you could hear a pin drop. I walked back into the room with my Mom. The Doctor came in. She asked me, "Do you have a boyfriend, Meagan?" With an almost locked jaw, *"No ma'am."*

Her voice started cracking, and she said: *"Well I sure hope so... because you're pregnant and you need to tell him!"* My Mom said nothing. She closed her mouth tight, and tears ran down her cheeks. Rocking front to back, she said looking at the Doctor, *"My baby is having a baby... Oh my Godddd!"* That was that. She knew now. I was 13 and pregnant.

I thought my Mom would disown me. I knew she was sick of my shit, on top of that now I had the nerve to be pregnant. Thirteen years old at that! Thirteen going on thirty-three. My Mom did the complete opposite of what I thought. Man, she was so sweet and supportive. Til' this day, I don't think she knows how much that meant to me at the time. Being that young, going through what I was going through. Now just imagine how many other girls went through this same situation who had no support and was torn down by the people they thought would support them or had no resources. To think about what they experienced hurts me. It could've been so much worse for me.

I begged my Mom not to tell GiGi or my brother and sisters. None of the family. She promised it would stay our little secret. I still can't believe how much about that day and that time of my life that I remember so clearly. It really was life-changing. When we walked back to the car and drove off, that was when my Mom started asking questions. She wanted to know who the baby's dad was, where this happened, whether or not I wanted to keep it... everything.

"*No!*" *That* was my immediate answer. If I could've gotten away with yelling *Hell no!* I would have because that's really what I thought she wanted to hear. You have no idea how good of a feeling it was for me to hear those comforting words from my Mom, who I just knew didn't want shit to do with me,

"Meagan you don't have to if you don't want to. I would never force you to do something like that. I would never let anybody else force you to do something like that! This is still your body, your baby and your decision. It's up to you baby. I love you, and I'm here for you no matter what you do. You hear me?"

I instantly felt safe. Support goes a long way for kids. That's exactly what I was, a kid. Regardless of the situation, regardless of how mature I was, at the end of the day, I was her child first. I felt like everything was going to be ok after that conversation. The pressure was off... I thought.

Since I already knew I was pregnant, and so did SAJ, I waited on him to call, and I told him what happened. SAJ was just as scared as I was about this baby but he didn't have a problem with whatever choice I made. One thing we did know for a fact was we couldn't tell anybody that he was the Dad. Not even my Mom. SAJ had turned 18 a few months ago, and I was a little over three months. He was fighting a drug case, and the last thing I wanted for him was a rape charge. I was underage as hell.

He didn't have any kids so the child I was carrying would have been the first for us both. I loved him so much; I wanted to keep our baby. I don't think I'd ever been so frustrated before in my life until then. I didn't know what to do! In a matter of only months, this boy has taken my virginity, stole my whole heart, not half and had gotten me pregnant. He was everything to me, as anybody could imagine, I was willing to do whatever I needed to protect him.

This is where Josh came into play. Josh was like my fake boyfriend from the YMCA. All we'd ever done was kiss on the side of the building. We were more friends than anything. Nothing special, crazy or big but we were friends right? I needed a baby daddy to fill in, and he was the guy. Josh, like many guys in East Columbus at that time, had a lot of respect for SAJ, if not terrified of him. He had made a name for himself everywhere through the city, and people knew of him. I used that to my advantage when finding this baby daddy fill in.

Ok, I did the absolute most asking Josh to do this for me. Even going so far as to say SAJ asked if Josh would do us a favor. SAJ didn't even know who Josh was! Whatever I ended up saying to Josh, he agreed. He was down! I actually still owe him a few dollars today because Lord did I put him through it. Accidentally! Yes, the Dr. had contacted Children's Services who sent out a private detective to look into the details of the case since I was so young. This caught my Mom and me off guard. Especially me!

I had to get my story together and quick! I felt so bad because I had to throw Josh under the bus. He hadn't signed up for all this extra shit. Trying to be my friend, he'd damn near went from a star football player at his High School, to almost in trouble now for having sex with me. Which in reality, he'd never done. Word spread quickly that I was pregnant and people were talking. Somebody at my previous school, Mifflin Middle, told the detective who went to question my old classmates that I talked about somebody older, named Saj a lot.

He was more than likely the Dad and that I was lying about Josh. Hunnie, Josh's Mom wasn't having it either. The spot was getting hot, and all I knew was that this baby had to go...now! My heart was broken when my Mom told me we were going to have to tell GiGi because we needed her to pay for the abortion. All that sweet, innocent baby girl, Grandma's favorite was on it's way out the window!

It was almost that time, and I was going to have to be a big girl to get through it. I was going to have to be strong whether I could handle it or not. We pulled up and the first thing I noticed was all the protesters standing outside. I remember pulling in and looking out the passenger seat window at angry faces holding poster boards with pictures, very graphic pictures of aborted babies. I was getting sick. Butterflies. Sweating! It was dead winter outside, and I was hot as hell.

A Staff from the doctor's office came and grabbed us from the car, and we went into the lobby. It was so nice and quiet inside. Waterfalls and soft music playing in the background. Nothing but adult women surrounded me getting their paperwork done. My Mom grabbed mine, and we waited. Going through something as serious as an abortion at thirteen years old, was not easy and was extremely emotional for me. I don't regret anything, but I think about those days often.

Even now. Once I got to the back and laid on the bed, I started to feel like I was having a bad dream. The room was freezing, looked creepy with all these tools laid out on a metal table; it was so intimidating. The nurse hooked me up to my anesthesia IV, and seconds later, I was out. The last thing I remember was one of the nurses tripping over my IV cord which ended up pulling at my arm. Oh no, she didn't apologize either! When I woke up, I was in recovery. My Mom was all I could see when I opened my eyes. She gets the "Mom of a lifetime award" for having my back the way she did throughout that process. I could not have done it without her, that's for damn sure.

Rebellious

Thought I knew everything. I was off the porch early. Even though I was too young to have lost my virginity, I wouldn't say that I was *fast*. Until I was off into High School, SAJ was all I had known. I never chased boys or got into trouble for *being too grown* in the sense of being disrespectful to adults or wearing clothes that showed too much... etc. I was always just way ahead of my time. One day I was helping my Mom clean her house and came across a letter my 5th-grade teacher had written to me when I left her going to middle school.

In the letter, she wrote, "Sometimes I forget you're just a kid." That wasn't hard to do. Even as a young girl I carried myself a certain way. I was that 8th-grade student with a red rinse and a roller wrap, referring my teachers to my beautician. My classmates had ponytails and braids. As I mentioned, my Mom was supportive of anything her kids wanted to pursue, she was a great provider to all of us, and she was overprotective when it came to things like whose house she allowed us to go over when we were younger.

She just wasn't so far off in our little business that she was aware of everything or prevented us from doing a lot of the things we went out and did on our own. I honestly believe as a parent, especially as a single Mother, that there's only so much that you can do to ensure success from your child. You can show them right from wrong, and you can teach them what you want them to know, but once you've done your job, it's ultimately up to each child to act on what you've done and said. They'll make their own choices. From thirteen to fifteen, I spent a lot of months in and out of juvenile detention centers because I wanted to do things how I wanted to do them.

Eventually, my Mom got sick of me and stopped coming to pull me out of holes I'd gotten myself into. The difference is, some kids aren't given a choice from good and bad or right and wrong because of how they're raised. Kids pay attention and pick up on *what you show them not what you tell them*. If you *tell* them don't do this, don't do that, but they *see you* doing it, it's going to almost be impossible to convince them that what you're doing isn't something they should do themselves. I mean why not? Mom is doing it. Dad is doing it. It must be ok.

Then you have some people who grow up ignorant, procrastinators, lazy, troubled, rude, etc. because that's what they saw growing up. It doesn't even feel wrong when they're doing it because they don't know anything outside of that. You have people who grow up to be hustlers, well spoken, well rounded and so on because that's how *they* were raised. That's what *they* grew up seeing. Have you ever seen a family with generations of failure or success? Only doing what they have seen before.

By the time I was born, I think my Mom's wildest years were over for the most part. When my Mom was sentenced and went to prison, at that time, I didn't understand why she had to leave us. But as I got older, some of the things that were going on started to make more sense. She never went back to the FEDS at any other point after that when I was growing up, but I did watch my Mom battle certain addictions. The streets. It was like she couldn't leave them alone. Four kids and all, my Mom never took the legal route my whole life.

She did what she knew to do. Run a street pharmacy. Before then, she was a pimp. I think she told me Tiffany's Dad was her driver for the operation she ran. A couple of years ago, my Mom told me all about it. She said while she was in prison, she met an Asian lady who gave her the game. When she was released, she took her Welfare check, flipped it and never looked back. All of her bests of friends we knew... in the streets too. They weren't *bad* people, I wouldn't say we ever were in any real danger, but this is what I grew up in. It was normal.

My life was two-sided though because my Mom gave us the best of everything she could. So even though I knew she was struggling while doing it, considering *what* she was doing to make it happen, none of us, the kids, were affected by it in a bad way. Meaning, there was never a day I came into our house, and the lights were off. There was never days and days of us having no food in the fridge. As a matter of fact, we always had *two* refrigerators full of shit. Now she may have gone to some food pantries, got some food stamps, bought some food stamps and sold some pills to make sure of that, but that's what it was.

I didn't grow up messed up; I just grew up fast. It takes a certain type of smart for a woman to go through struggles that their children don't. When people provide for their families like that, it takes time away, and it drains them. There was never any sitting down with us and doing homework. She would hire a tutor. There was never any dinners where we all sat down to the table and ate as a family. There weren't times when she pulled me to the side and had talks that other kids my age were having with their parents. She never came to parent-teacher conferences. I can count how many whoppings I ever got; she just didn't have *time* to do things like that. My Mom didn't sugar coat anything! Like I *always* knew, there wasn't any Santa Claus. She told us Christmas was whenever she had some money. If she was fucked up December 25th and was up in June, Christmas was in June.

My Mom was a realist with us. Period. She hustled *with* her kids. Once she got rid of our Nanny long before, there was never any more babysitters. We came *with* her to hit her stings and when she would go to Compton and cop her shit. We'd stay at home by ourselves. If we didn't, we were with GiGi in Lynwood or at Auntie Michelle's house in Centerview. Diane didn't baby us, ever. There were things now looking back, that she shouldn't have been doing in front of us, but she did it. I watched her, and I took note. So regardless of anything I got *told* by anybody else, *that's* what I grew up *seeing – every day*. That's what created my character. I was grown as hell by default. Whole childhood skipped.

Chapter 3

SHE'S DEAD

Taneisha is the oldest of my Mom's four. She had every feature a girl could want. Light brown skin. Hazel, almond-shaped eyes. Long honey blonde and brown hair. She had this gap in the middle of her teeth, her two front ones, and a mole on the right side of her face, above her top lip. You know that one beauty mark we would all draw on with lip liner as kids. Taneisha was so pretty; she had a smile that would literally brighten up a whole room. Her whole aura, energy, and spirit was beautiful. I was so blessed to be able to enjoy 15yrs. with her. We have the best memories together. Losing her was another test of my strength. Just when I thought I could handle anything, my world was torn into pieces within hours.

June 2007, my Mom flew us into Los Angeles for a family vacation and to attend my brother's High School graduation. We got to California, and over to my Auntie Michelle's house, everybody was so excited to see us! It had been years since we were all in the same place, in that house like that. The family had cooked, and we all ate, talked, laughed and messed around all night with each other like we use to. We were there a few days before, and today it was graduation day for Quentin. Me, Mommy, Auntie Michelle, and Taneisha all rode from Carson to Rancho Cucamonga.

A 1:20 minutes' drive, for some reason took us all day. Like several hours! Traffic was insane, and we got lost! By the time we made it, the entire parking lot was pulling out from the stadium as we were pulling in. My brother was pissed! As if his relationship with Mom could get any more distant, we had missed the whole ceremony. I can appreciate us getting lost now because what I didn't know was those were our last hours together.

So I look at it as I was just given more time with my baby. When my sister was twelve weeks old, my Mom found out Taneisha had Epilepsy. Her Epilepsy caused her to have seizures. She had been getting treated for it her entire life. She also had Schizophrenia, which would cause her to hear voices that nobody else did. It was really bad if her medication was off or "set off" by something. This whole day Taneisha's voices were bad. Real bad. She talked us to death about all types of shit. We left the stadium parking lot and stopped up the street at a 7Eleven so that everybody could use the restroom before getting back on the road to my Aunt's house. This was when things started to get angelic to me once I looked back on this night.

Mom was helping Taneisha out of the car; they walked into the gas station. I was trailing behind them, going in to get snacks and pay for the gas. As I was walking up to the sliding doors, I saw a lady standing there by the entrance. It looked like she was asking people for change. You know normally when that's the case, they'll wait until you're coming out of the store before they ask for anything. I was standing in the line holding my blueberry muffin and Funyuns, already thinking about how I could dodge her asking me for anything.

When I came out, she wasn't standing there anymore. I got back to the car and saw my Aunt hugging and rubbing the back of someone who was standing on the side of our car crying. It's the same lady! I started the pump and got in the car. I was still trying to ignore this woman and get my Aunt to stop talking to her because I couldn't imagine what the hell she could have wanted from us. A ride? I don't know. I was taught always to give people asking for change, whatever money I could when I see them, so it wasn't that.

I just didn't have anything for her, her crying had me irritated, and Taneisha already had been talking us down all day and night. I wasn't in the mood. After a while, I actually began listening to what this lady was saying, and I thought she was a creep! Here she was telling my Aunt how much she appreciates and respects my Mom for taking such good care of Taneisha and how blessed she was going to be. God sees all her hard work and the efforts she puts into the wellbeing of my sister... I mean she went on and on.

The lady told my Aunt she too has a daughter with epilepsy, who has "drop seizures." Drop seizures are VERY dangerous. People like my sister, who have drop seizures are not ever to be left alone for long periods of time. She said her daughter was at home down the street and she had to hurry up and get back to her. All I could think was if your daughter has seizures like that, why the fuck would you leave her there alone anyway? And how do you know if my Mom takes good care of my sister or not? You don't even know us! Beat it.

That's what I really wanted to say, but before we could fully respond to what she was saying, this lady had hurried up and said she had to go, had walked around the other side, behind the trunk and disappeared. Literally. Gone. Auntie Michelle said she'd told the lady to wait a second for my Mom and Taneisha to come back out so that my Mom could advise her on the best meds to take to control her daughter's drop seizures. She still kept saying she had to go. Mom and Taneisha were walking up to the car to get in, and me and my Aunt started telling my Mom about the lady.

We didn't realize she had completely vanished until my Mom said "Oh ok, where'd she go? I saw her at the door when we walked in." We looked front, back, side to side but she was nowhere in sight! My Mom put the car in reverse to pull out but was still turning her head looking for this woman so she wouldn't hit her if she was walking up again. No lady in sight! We got out into the middle of the street; my Mom looked over to the other side of the hill to see if we'd see her speed walking or running. Nowhere visible was there any signs of this lady. "Where the hell did she just go that fast?" My Aunt said exactly what I was thinking. We kept on down the road, and that was that. We thought nothing else of it. It was so weird.

"Yall hungry?" My Mom said. "Yeah, can we go to Jack-N-The Box?" That was what Taneisha asked. "Oh my Godddd!" I was pissed! We were making another stop! I was so ready to get back to the house. I didn't feel like riding all the way out there in the first place. We got our food and were finally on the highway. My Mom dropped us all back at Auntie Michelle's house. "Meagan, keep an eye on Taneisha, I'll be back." "Ok." I had no intentions of keeping no extra eyes on anybody. It's a house full of my Aunts and cousins; she'll be fine. I was tired and annoyed by the time we'd got to Carson.

I grabbed my charger, attached my pink T-Mobile Razor phone to it and called Fatty back. He'd been texting me the whole ride, but I told him I would call him when I got in the house so I could hear. I sat on the phone with him all night long, until the sun was on its way up. I fell asleep just like that. Every time we'd talk or got together that's just what it was with us. He changed my shitty attitude I had all day and had me smiling ear to ear.

It had to be like 6, maybe 7 in the morning. Grandmommy had just gotten home from work, doing her usual, cleaning. Getting the house in order. My cousins were up getting ready for school; my Mom came in. She used the restroom and walked to the back into Grand mommy's room to wake Taneisha up to use the restroom too. My Mom had no idea that when she left out to kick it and have a good time with her friends, when she kissed her daughter goodnight, that she was really kissing her goodbye. *Here Taneisha, get up. You're wet.* My Mom turned Taneisha over off her stomach and when she rolled over onto her back, all you heard after that were loud yells and screams. *Ahhhhhhh!!* Yelling, screaming. *Noooo, my God!!! Please no!!! Jesus please no!!! Come on baby wake up Neisha! Get up! Lord what is this!? What is going on!? Wake up baby!*

My cousin Brittany came running into the living room where I was knocked out sleeping with my phone in my hand. *Meagan get up! Taneisha had a seizure!* I'm thinking like, "Okay." I went back to sleep. Taneisha has been having seizures my whole life. I know what they look like. I know what they cause. I know what to expect from them. If she had a seizure, you all know what to do too, there's no reason for me to get up and walk to the back of the house when we all know what to do. I've been up all night on the phone; I'm tired!

Those were my thoughts as I laid there. That's the most I was thinking. It's a blur to me who came in next, but they screamed, *Meagan you need to get up now! Something is wrong with your sister! She's not breathing!* My fucking heart dropped to my feet! I jumped up and ran to the back! I didn't have my contacts in so my eyesight wasn't clear at all. I could barely see anything. When I got to the bedroom door, I saw my Mom sitting high up on the bed, with Taneisha's head between her legs. She was holding my sister's face, shaking her, screaming and crying *My baby is gone!!!* I got into the bed, beside her. I had to get close even to see what was going on.

I'd never been that close to a dead body, so I didn't really know what I was looking for, but all I did know was my sister looked *lifeless*. I started slapping her face, begging her to wake up. Everything felt like it was racing. Heart beating faster than it ever had. I was so scared. I was sweating and couldn't breathe. Her pretty face was light purple, her lips a dark purple color. I squeezed her hand; it didn't budge. How long is it going to take for my sister to wake back up? There ain't no fucking way this is it for us.

My Mom can't live without Taneisha; she's all she knows. My sister *is* her life. This is 34 years of unconditional love laying in her arms. The ambulance rushed in and carried Taneisha from the bed into the living room. They laid her flat on her back on the floor. They pumped her chest continuously with their defibrillators for at least three to six minutes. I watched her body lift off the ground an inch every time. One of the medics was on his walkie reading off her heart rate to the operator. I felt a tiny bit of relief but still scared out of my mind. It's like, I still can't even find the words to describe this day in detail in a way anybody would understand.

The medics took Taneisha, and my Mom rode with them in the truck. I got to the hospital maybe 15 to 20 minutes later. I remember getting into the lobby and asking the woman at the counter which way was Taneisha Pitchford; she told me to have a seat. Wrong answer. I lost it instantly! A seat? She couldn't be serious. I blacked out. When I opened my eyes, I was on the ground. A tall, bald, black security officer stood over me. "I need you to please calm down! I don't want to arrest you! Please, calm down. It's going to be ok, I promise you. Everything is going to be ok. You can't do this in here."

He held me like that restrained for about ten minutes. "Family for Ms. Pitchford?" A nurse yelled. "You can follow me. Please be quiet; there are a lot of sick people back here. This is the ICU." She pointed me in the direction to where they were. I pulled back that blue curtain and saw

Taneisha lying in bed, my Mom sitting in a chair next to her, running her finger through her hair.

I could finally smile, I just knew she'd made it fine. She looked asleep. She looked so peaceful. "She's ok now?" I asked my Mom. "No Meagan. She's gone baby, I'm sorry." Tears were coming down my Mom's cheeks. Her eyes were red. Lashes wet. I couldn't believe how everybody had lied to me! The heart rate that the medics read out loud was all fake. My baby had been dead hours before my Mom even walked into that room and found her. She was gone and was never coming back.

Everything made sense to me after a while. That lady from 7Eleven wasn't a panhandler or a creep; she was an angel. God had sent her to tell my Mom, "Good job, well done." If nothing else, my Mom definitely deserved to hear that and to know all she'd done for her kids, especially Taneisha, didn't go unnoticed or unappreciated. That lady wasn't crying for no reason. Those tears she shed were for my Mom. As crazy as it sounds, I didn't see my Mom doing too much breaking down crying, and I honestly believe that's why. Taneisha's voices were bad like that, that whole day and night because she was being spoken to. God was preparing her for the transition she was about to make, and she couldn't keep quiet about it. She kept saying "Mama you proud of me? The Devil tried to get me to go with him, but I told him I was God's child! I'm a child of God, huh? Ain't I? You proud of me?" I'm talking about she got on our nerves that day saying that over and over again! I didn't know what the hell she was talking about. I just thought she was rambling. We all kept saying "Yes! Yes, Taneisha she's proud of you. We're *all* proud of you!" Hmph, funny how things work. My sister knew she was about to leave us and she was ready. As young as she was, her purpose in life had been served, and she was ready to go back home. He was ready for her. *We* weren't.

I remember my cousin Kymberli calling her Mom and telling her what happened that morning. She could barely get the words out of her mouth before my Aunt hung up in her face. All I heard was her yell "What!!?" It wasn't until days later that my Auntie Michelle came back home. I didn't know where she was or what she was doing, but I was so worried about her. She loved Taneisha so much! I was praying at night for her to come back safe. It wasn't but the night before that we were all together in the car riding around for hours with each other.

Her last hours of life were spent with us. It was some shit we just couldn't wrap our minds around and didn't want to. I was so happy to finally see my Aunt's face when she walked through that door. She'd been through so much in her life, from battling drug addictions and so on. The last thing I wanted was for this loss to take her back to a stage she has passed. Today my Aunt is clean. Of everything, her testimony gives me chills and inspires me in ways I know she knows nothing about. She made that time in my life easier to deal with. She kept me calm. She prayed with me but most importantly, when I wasn't around, she was praying *for* me. I needed that.

Being fifteen years old and planning an entire funeral damned nearby yourself takes a lot from you. Can you even imagine that? Everything from the obituary outline to picking out caskets, looking for what outfit my sister would be buried in, meeting with funeral directors to picking music... I was front row center. Though it was ten grand of GiGi's money being spent, I was the one doing all the planning and decision making. The baby sister. What happened during all this is the reason why till this day, I'm cool on Quentin. That's my brother.

I'll never forget or forgive the way he acted. The weird vibes he gave off. From when we'd gotten back from the hospital to the day of the funeral, he acted like he could care less, he wasn't affected and didn't really want to be involved in anything we were doing. When my Mom called him to tell him Taneisha died, he told her he would call her back; he was at his senior breakfast! That alone was enough disrespect towards my Mom (which by the way is his blood Mother too) and my sister to never speak to him again.

I wanted to do more than that, but my focus was somewhere else. To make it worse, when he found out he was listed as a pallbearer, he was pissed! Who wouldn't want the honor of carrying their sister at her service!? This is it anyway! Death is as final as anything will ever get. Whether you grew up in the same household with us or not, there are certain things you don't do to family. To me, that shit was evil. It's been eleven years, and I still feel the same way. So I guess our relationship is what it's going to be.

The whole service was beautiful in the end. I stood up at the front of the church right next to my sister's casket the whole time with my head held high. I knew then that I had a type of strength that was unmatched. If I could handle losing my heart, regretting not doing more while she was here and carrying out a whole funeral at fifteen, I could deal with whatever life planned to throw at me. When we went to view her to make sure everything looked good, I remember being so nervous to walk into the funeral home.

GiGi, my Mom, and Auntie Michelle went in while I sat outside in the car for like 45 minutes. My Aunt came out to ask me to come in and see how beautiful Taneisha looked, the smell that hit my face, stuck to my skin for months seemed like. I couldn't get that smell out of my mind. I would scrub my face harder each time I washed it trying to get rid of this smell under my nose, not realizing it was a mental thing – all in my head.

The night before, while I was on the phone with Fatty, my Mom called me on the other line and said *Meagan get up and go check on Taneisha. Make sure she went to the bathroom*, "Ok." *Now! For real Meagan. Do it NOW!* I didn't. Not too long before she called I'd just left from back there telling Taneisha to go lay down. She was up all night. Late as hell! Walking around to every room my cousins and me were in and just stood there staring. I take that now as her saying her goodbyes to us. They say people can feel death when it's on its way. That was the last time I saw my sister alive. June 13, 2007.

Chapter 4

WELCOME TO ATLANTA

I'd been traveling back and forth to Atlanta from Ohio for a little over a year. When I say back and forth, I mean like literally every other week I was hopping on a flight into the city. My homegirl lived there, she would grab me from the airport, and I would stay at her house. Being from Los Angeles and always going home to visit as I got older, you'd think there wasn't anything fly or fancy I hadn't already seen or been exposed to, but what I got from Atlanta was just different. I fell in love with the city quickly. I don't know why, but every time I landed, I'd feel like I was *home*. I don't even get that feeling when landing in LA.

It was something about the energy I got, the atmosphere and the people I met. It did it for me. Real good vibes. It began to make me realize how negative of a space Columbus, Ohio was. Like a dark cloud covered it and as soon as I got outside of there, I was happier. Everybody I would meet was telling me to move to the city, and I hated leaving when going back. Just like it felt like home, the people I was meeting treated me like I was family. Even with a lot of them being industry friends. I don't look at them like that. All this time later, with most of them, we're still like family. Nobody is like that where I'm from. Not in California and damned sure not in Ohio.

As you probably already know, cities like Houston, Miami, Chicago, Los Angeles, and Atlanta are vacation spots for some, but for others, they are cities with better opportunities for them, so there tends to be a lot of people who've migrated there. Others move for peace of mind away from what's going on where they're living. So there was definitely a lot going on, and I wanted in. After my first time visiting, I knew that Atlanta was exactly where I wanted to be, for good. I didn't wait for the opportunity to present itself either. I didn't wait for the perfect time. I created my own and ran with it.

September 2010, my friend was murdered in a double-homicide in East Columbus. At the time I was working at Discover Card as a Customer Service Rep. His death, to say the least, made me rethink a lot about my life. I felt like his life was so short-lived, and he didn't deserve to go the way he did or as soon as he did. I felt like if given a chance, he could have been one of the greatest at whatever he chose to do. But instead of it going how it should have, this coward Levander took that choice away from Tyejuan at only 17yrs old.

I was just like, damn. Do I want to sit around in Columbus and keep watching this happen to people I know and love or do I want to go somewhere I love being and get more out of life myself? That way I could show them it's possible instead of preaching it to them. I can lead by example and hopefully encourage and inspire them to do the same. I kept being told *Meagan you have already outgrown this city as young as you are*. Think about what I'd do down there with everything I need in arms reach. All the resources and support.

The people I'd dealt with and the friends I had in Atlanta all wanted to see me win. *Fuck this! I'm leaving!* Wasn't a damn thing going on in Ohio but murders, drama, prison sentences and trips to labor and delivery. I was over it! To add to the devastation I was dealing with, in that same month, our house burned down. We lost basically everything. My Mom said she wasn't looking for anywhere else to live in Columbus. She said she was moving back to Cali and I was welcomed to come. I chose not to. I knew where I was going. This only made my decision that much easier.

I put in a leave at Discover Card, took the couple thousand I had in my account and got the hell on! The guy who I was dealing with at the time would have me to keep every paycheck I got and put it up, not to be touched. He gave me money for my day to day living expenses, so I was never touching any of my own money for almost two years. When I left, for a while I was good with what I had. We were together or dealt with each other on and off over the years. It was always a problem with his baby mother. What he didn't know was towards the end, I'd already known I was done and was making sure I'd be just fine without him when I got ready.

I really believed that things couldn't get any worse than what SAJ had put me through as a young girl, so I would keep certain guards up with boys and always was aware and paying attention to everything going on. He was seven years older than me, so some things he got over on. Cutting him completely off and walking away from that situation came sooner than I thought when one night he tried to kill me.

This night, Shanice had dropped me off to him at the Super8. The two of us spent a lot of time there together over the past few years because the Super8 is where he would hustle out of. On any given night, there was sometimes a line outside his room door of people there to cop. All through the night, people were knocking on the door. I guess those are the chances you take when you're in love because I was clearly sitting in a fed case 95% of the time when I was with him. I mean he'd have every drug you can think of in the room, hidden in the walls and ceiling. This was every single night. Guns, large amounts of cash if we hadn't taken it to be put up... for years! Here I was just wanting to be around him, that's what came with it. Risks.

The front desk staff and housekeepers were all on his payroll. They would clean *around* his dope and call him when officers were anywhere near. Never one mishap. This night was no different. Everything was normal until he broke down this pill and snorted it. In front of us! I was pissed! Me and Shanice looked at each other shocked! Did he really just snort a line in my fucking face!? Note you, I'd known him for *years* and had never ever seen him do anything like that! He'd smoke his weed and drink his liquor, but that's it. Hard drugs or pills was nothing he'd ever done around me or spoke of around me. Shanice ended up leaving.

Of course, I stayed with him. It started with me cursing him out and going off about him doing drugs; our argument led from one thing to the other, and we started fighting. Fist fighting! Tussling. Pushing. Throwing. Breaking. He had never before put his hands on me. This night he was extremely aggressive! The look in his eyes made it real clear to me that he was dead ass serious, he *will* hurt me and will *not* care how this ends. Before I knew it, Blow had grabbed his gun, cocked it back and put it in my face. It was like everything had stopped. I stood there crying, looked at the bullet that was in the barrel and just closed my eyes.

I thought it was the fuck over. For sure! He went to press down on the trigger of the gun, and it was jammed. At the same time I was opening my eyes, he was throwing his arm back. Boom! He slapped me so hard with that gun on my mouth and it bust instantly. I flew in between the table and bed. I laid there for a minute with my eyes closed. I could just hear him moving around. A few minutes later I heard sirens. Somebody had called the ambulance. Thank God! I got up and ran out of the room, down the stairs and was flagging down the trucks as they pulled in the parking lot. They gave me something for my mouth, but I refused to go to the ER.

The police actually dropped me off to GiGi's, in Pickerington. When I got there, she wasn't there. I had my cell phone but it was dead. I sat outside her door on the steps and broke down. I could barely move my face when I was crying because of how swollen it had gotten. My shirt was ripped. My hair was all over my head. He'd pulled it out in some parts. I was hot, weak and in pain. I felt so fucking low; betrayed isn't the word. My heart was in a million pieces. This man had done me so dirty. Now I'm sitting here looking crazy with nowhere to go. Not literally nowhere to go, but nowhere I wanted to go and be seen the way I was looking then have to worry about explaining what the hell happened to me.

I got up and started walking down Refugee Rd. towards Hill Rd. LaDarius's parents lived near the police station. I'd been over there a couple of times before, but not in a long time. I don't know what made me go over there in the middle of the night, but I was just like fuck it, pride going to the side! I needed to get somewhere safe and clean, so I could finally go to sleep. I didn't want them to see me like that, as a matter of fact, they were the *last* people I wanted to see me like that but they lived right down the street from GiGi's and they were older, so it's not like they were about to jump on the phone and start gossiping about it.

They opened the door for, didn't look at me weird, and didn't make me feel bad. They welcomed me right in and just asked if I was I ok. Mr. Alexander went and got me a few blankets and pillows, made a pallet for me on the floor, Mrs. Toya made me a sandwich, and I laid there until I fell asleep. I never told the police what happened and he was never arrested for it. I just knew from that day forward he was dead to me. It was over with! There was nothing I can say that I even wanted to be done to him physically, but as I kept thinking about the shit he was saying to me and the way he made me feel, it motivated me. It made me feel like I had a lot of shitting on him to do.

I could have done to him whatever I wanted given the circle I was in, but I swear I didn't want any of that. I could say whatever I wanted to him, but it would have gone in through one ear and out the other. What I knew for sure that would have him feeling the way I wanted him to feel was to do everything I said I was going to do – leave Columbus for good. Go to Atlanta and get myself together. After what happened to me, I couldn't get going fast enough. I was going to make sure that everybody who had something to say; anybody who doubted or played me who I thought was close, would start to feel like outsiders as they watched me progress from a distance.

I wanted him to feel like an outsider. I wanted him first hand, to witness how I only got better and how I had taken what I knew, what I learned and applied it to my life. How smart I'd trained myself to be. I'm always a student. If I look like I'm not paying attention, know that I am. I wanted him to see me and be like damn, *what I did to break her created a fucking monster in beast mode*. Brag about what you *had*, because I'm done.

I hadn't seen my new place in person yet or anything! But that deposit was paid, and my keys were ready when I got back to Atlanta. Who doesn't do walk-throughs? That's how pressed, and in a hurry I was to move! I had told my Mom I was ready to move there for college. So that's what she thought I was doing – getting me a place to live while I went to school at Clark. We toured the campus not too long ago, and I told her that's where I was going... I never attended one day of college in my life. But you couldn't tell me nothin'. I was gone! I left that nigga in Columbus, and I was exactly where I wanted to be! My very first apartment. It was a beautiful new build.

At one point during my back and forth escapades to Atlanta, I'd met Gizelle. We met through mutual friends. You ever met somebody who you clicked with so much, that every time you got around them, you thought *where the hell have you been all my life?* That's how I was with her. Once me and her linked it was over. It was like we grew up together, we got so close. Even though the lives me and Gizelle lived day to day were the complete opposite, the two of us together balanced it all out.

What I wasn't, she was, and what she wasn't, I was. That's just how we clicked. Like sisters. She was about her bag and was fun to be around. One of the funniest people you'll ever meet. The biggest difference between us I would have to say was the fact that she was a pornstar and I was.... wasn't. The things she had going on was nothing I was used to. I just never judged her or anything she did because I knew her overall intentions. I knew her plans, and I knew her outside of what other people seen.

I had a lot of respect for Gizelle as a friend, and she definitely had the same for me. It's important to have people like that in your life. People that you trust and can be you around, and they accept it. Never anything shady. Even if they are shooting porn during the day and you're living a regular life, waiting on them to get done with a scene so you two can go get lunch and Patron together at your favorite Mexican restaurant.

That was our life. Work, kick it. Do it again the next day. Me and this girl lived our best lives together that's for damn sure, those stories I'll save for another book that she can tell herself. For about two years straight we were partying. But never without profit. Gizelle at that time was at the height of her career as an adult entertainer. Trending on WorldStar and booked every week in a different city. She would either go host a club or would dance.

Instead of just having me come with her and party, she asked me to be her Road Manager. It was like a verbal agreement we had with each other. She knew I was good with negotiating, speaking and handling the business aspect of things and we were already together all the time, so it only made sense. Over that period, we traveled to a bunch of different cities. Hostings, radio interviews, shooting, filming. Just the two of us. We made money together, as a team. A lot. My friend never short-handed me or didn't give me more than I was worth. I'll love her forever for that.

At night when we'd be back at the hotel after a show, sitting on the floor counting money, she'd still split her back-end with me in one way or the other. None of my negotiations with those promoters or club owners went in vain. We looked out for each other, no matter what. She's that friend who was Googling net worths before storing numbers in her phone. A fool! My girl did not play, not one game. Hilarious!

I've seen a lot of females do for free what she did for some people's salaries, so I never once looked down on her. Of course, I wanted different for her because I knew how great of a woman she was and seen in her more than she had probably seen in herself back then, but I remained solid through everything we did. I'm that friend that's like *"girl, you can do what he's doing your damned self, and faster, they're the underdogs we're the ones with the power."* I knew the day that she decided to move on was coming, but we enjoyed *every* minute of what things were, while we were living it.

One morning, I woke up and had like four missed calls from Gizelle. I opened up her text, and she said: *Go to MediaTakeOut right now!* Oh hell no! The headline read, "Threesome gone wrong! Rapper Young Dro gets into trouble". Then the name dropping began. The lies spread from one blog to the next. There were only two, maybe three people who knew about this situation and knew what happened but not in detail. So of course, all I could think of was who the hell sent this story in? We blamed other people but were still like *who did this, was it you bitch?* People were telling me she sent the story in for publicity, just like I'm sure people were telling her the same thing, but it didn't make either one of us look good.

Everybody had something to say that week. My relationship with Gizelle just got weird after that, and I hated it. I wouldn't say mine, and his changed for the worse. We talked about some stuff and laughed about the rest later, but that's it. He was always good to me for the most part. My throwed off buddy from Bankhead. What went on between the three of us put a strain on Gizelle and me, and it was almost nine or ten months before we spoke again. We didn't even fall out. I don't know what the hell all that mess was those websites were talking about; we just stopped communicating. You can't put molly in your mouth and have sex with two people you love, too many feelings involved. I won't even go into detail about what all happened, but I will say it hasn't been another night like it.

Me and Gizelle ended up linking back up in Miami. She had been there for a minute shooting for her website, and I'd come for vacation but ended up talking to her on my way headed back home. She pulled up on me literally *at* the airport, and I didn't leave Miami until a month later. We had the time of our lives out there. The best make up!

After Miami, we were back working together. Only by then, I'd started my own business, so I was super busy! Anything she could do to help grow my business and support it, she did. We got back home and would really sit down and have brainstorming sessions with each other about how to grow our brands. We were both doing so good in what we were doing.

It's something about watching people you actually know, set goals and achieve them. The people I associated myself with were all doing something with theirselves. Great things. Everybody's homes and condos were beautiful. Many had fifty and eighty thousand dollar cars – all under 30. I had my own vision and was motivated. There was no *go settle for a basic life and only get what they're willing to give you*. It was *go get what I wanted and do everything* BIG.

I moved to Atlanta and met some amazing people. Overall, I realized my own potential simply by being surrounded by people who were being their best *them*. My whole mindset had changed since leaving Ohio. I refused to settle for anything less than the best, and I looked at things differently. Launching my business gave me something of my own to build, grow and focus on daily. Had I never been exposed to a certain way of living, I would have never wanted it for myself. You usually don't want things you've never experienced yourself.

That's why I've always encouraged others to travel outside of their city so that they can experience more, see differently and be inspired to get up every day and go get more. For some people, that'll never happen where they're at. You become accustomed, and that's it. I'm glad my Mom always traveled with us as kids because as soon as I got old enough to go on trips *alone*, I did. I didn't plan any of it; I just started going where I wanted to go. I got that type of "go spirit" from her. Moving down South by myself, with no family and only a couple of friends that I'd just met was something plenty of people would've never done or procrastinated decades to do. Sometimes you just gotta go! That was one of the best decisions I could've made for myself.

Chapter 5

THE POINT OF IT ALL

The year before I moved to Atlanta was when I met LaDarius, the summer of 2009. At Eastland Mall. I guess I shouldn't say *met* because I didn't give him the time of day. I really didn't. My best friend at the time, Shanice was talking to one of his friends, and we ended up seeing them both that day at the mall. I'm not sure if she was meeting him there or not, but Shanice had stopped to talk to them, I kept going. I saw LA and wasn't interested in holding any type of conversation with him. I had remembered LA's face from being out in the bars and after hour spots.

He was those one type of guys you'd see out who just had that "look." You know, like you should stay away from them. They're probably on some bullshit. For sure was carrying a gun... that type. He looked dangerous. Clearly, I was pissed when I got a phone call, and it was him on my line! When we were in the mall and she came back from talking to them, I told her to keep him away from me. I heard LA say *Who IS that? I need her!* I didn't want no parts! I hung up when he said his name and never answered him again. Not long after, I was with Shanice again and this time out South, at the corner store on 22nd and Livingston. She parked on the side of the store and went in to grab something. I stayed in the car.

Sure enough, who walked up to the window? *Damn that's how you do me? I ain't never been played like this. You must don't know who I am.* Inside, I was dying laughing but I kept a straight face. He opened the door and sat in the drivers seat. *Can I call you tonight, please?* "I guess,", *You gon' answer?* I smiled and started laughing. *Yes.* I rolled my eyes. I was thinking to myself *let me just give this boy a chance. He is not about to leave me alone.* He was so persistent. Better not waste my time.

He was so handsome; his deep dimples, smile and how sweet he was, attracted me to him. His consistency too. He was trying so hard, it was so cute coming from the type of boy he was. He called me right after Shanice pulled off! *Just making sure you wasn't playing me again, what y'all bout' to do?*, *Nothing. I'll call you later on if we do.* Here's Shanice, *Girl, he likes you!* She burst out laughing. *See what my brother talkin' about'!* From then, me and LaDarius would talk to each other all the time. I was only 16 I think, he was 18, 19, so the places we had to go and really spend time together the way we wanted to were limited.

We had places we could go, but it was either a lot going on over there, or it was his parents' house. Those were the choices. He damned sure wasn't allowed over my house. My Mom wasn't having it. We just wanted to be alone. I would go out South to see him in the neighborhood, he'd get in the car with me, and we would talk for hours about everything. On the phone it was worse, we would really fall asleep talking and wake each other up when the sun came up.

One weekend he came and stayed the night at Shanice's house with me. He kept me up all night laughing. He tried me a little bit, but he wasn't pushy at all. When I moved his hand, all he did was be like, *it's ok. Let me just hold you. Let's go to sleep.* Until morning, that's how we laid. Held on to each other like we never planned on letting go.

On our first date, we went to the movies at Easton. I remember sitting down in the theater and getting a charley horse in my leg. I was in so much pain. LaDarius rubbed my leg and foot until that movie ended! It was so cute me seeing him just put forth his all. All he knew to do at his age anyway. I could tell even with this just being a movie date, it was all out of the norm for him, but he did a good job playing it off. Young boys from the hood don't go on dates. He didn't even know what to do. Down at the concession stand when he asked me what I wanted, I remember thinking like, he *is nervous as hell*. I laughed to myself.

Still, every time I'd look over, I was like *Damn, but I like him*. He was trying to keep up with me, and I was trying to stay on his page. Oh, it worked because I was there, right behind him, everywhere. Our first time going out together I remember him getting into it with some guys who were all piled up in this white SUV. It had to be like nine of them. It started as an argument; I kept yelling from the car begging LA to get back in. These guys had jumped out of their truck and the fights started! It was a nightmare! Bapo and LA got into a fight with each other when we got back to the house. LA was so mad; Nobody was anywhere to be found when everything popped off. I told him he didn't have to ever worry about me going any place else with him again! I wasn't ready for all that rowdy shit.

Three, four months had passed, and me and LA were stuck up under each other. In love and we made love too. From the very first time we had sex, I couldn't believe the things he was doing to me. Things I didn't even know my body could do. This wasn't any dry humping and bumping young boys; this boy was making love to me. Like a grown man, every time.

I was at work on my lunch break and called LA's phone back to back. No answer. Finally, his cousin JD picked up and told me he was in jail. I had mixed feelings. Part of me was sad; the other was mad! Disappointed. He'd told me he loved being around me because I kept him out of trouble and that he wouldn't be out getting into anything. I was pissed that he lied to me. He was only in jail a couple of weeks, but while he was there, he lost his favorite person in the world... his cousin, Fat Daddy.

The way that played out was crazy. Me and LA talked about how it was almost like he had seen this coming right before he went to jail. It was me, Fat Daddy and LA sitting in the living room at their spot on Hildreth. We were watching a movie; LA was laying with his head on my lap, Fat Daddy was over on the couch across from us. I happened to look down, and LA had tears rolling down his face. He was staring at his cousin. I didn't say anything about it right then but later on, LA told me he didn't know why, but he was having visions of his cousin being murdered.

He told me he would lose his mind if anything ever were to happen to him and weird enough, as soon as he went to jail, that's exactly what happened. LA got out, but he was no longer the same boy that I had met. He was a completely different person after Fat Daddy got killed. Completely. He jumped right back on his bullshit.

It was a weekday, late at night and I got a call from Shanae. She told me somebody had just walked into where she was and told her LA just got shot. I told her it couldn't have been true because I'd *just* spoke to him. My heart was beating faster than I could think! I was shaking! So scared. Here I was calling him, and nobody was picking up. Shanae called me back and said her and Rell were on their way up to the hospital. It *was true*! LA was shot in his stomach and had gone from critical to stable condition after surgery.

I was getting the updates over the phone. I didn't want to go up there and see him like that. When they told me he was going to be ok, I was ok. I think maybe two days had passed before I came to the hospital. When I walked in, I saw him lying in the bed; his eyes were closed. I thought he was sleep. I whispered and asked his Mom if he was ok and she just nodded her head. She told me to come into the hallway, and she'd tell me what was going on. Mrs. Alexander told me he would be fine but right now, he was in a lot of pain and his road to recovery would be long. I stayed at the hospital that night and never left his side. During my stay with him, is when I started finding out about these other girls he was talking to. They *all* were packing out the lobby, coming to his room and calling every five minutes. There were so many girls, and I was confused.

I wanted to be mad, but I couldn't. He wouldn't let me out his sight. His Dad cut off all visits, and it was just us. LaDarius kept me next to him lying in that hospital bed for the entire time he was there. We woke up early in the mornings and went to physical therapy. I fed him his food, wiped his ass and prayed with him and his parents. Laughed, cried, argued. All I kept thinking was as soon as he got well, I was cutting him off. By then I was in my feelings over him, and I refused to play around!

I don't know how, but while all this was going on, I had found out that one of the females who I'd seen come up there, she was a older woman with a real hard look, a deep voice, *and a thick full beard*; man, just crazy. Oh, and he lived with her! All this time, the house I'd been picking him up from and dropping him off to, wasn't his sister's like he said. It was hers! I had heard it all! I didn't see how that was even possible as much as we were together, but you'd be surprised.

Not too long after, he was locked up again. This time he was sentenced to prison. He told me he wouldn't be home for a while. I was all types of disgusted! So of course, this time when he went to jail, it was over! I told him I was going to let all his girls hold him down through his sentence and I went on with my little life in Atlanta. I would write to him here and there, send some pictures, but I never went to see him. What I found out about him was enough for me. I just focused on myself. Back with my wall up, I didn't bother with anybody else.

Chapter 6

THE FLIP

Whatever city I visit, I ask around and do my research to find the most popular places for beauty services to go to. When I got to ATL, one of my homegirls told me to go to Peters St. to get my hair done. A new stylist named Ming, who did her hair, took me as a walk-in. I got to Peters St. later in the day, and as usual, it was jumpin'! Cars parked bumper to bumper all down the block. People out on the street talking, hanging, loud music playing from the lounges – a nice Atlanta vibe. As soon as I pulled up, I fell in love with the salon. It was nice.

The interior designs were so me. Extra girly! Everything was pink or bling. Vintage accents and wall art. It was new and the "go-to" beauty shop in the city at the time. They had more of the college girl clientele and was known for always having celebs pop in and out.

Something ended up being wrong with my hair that I didn't like and that's how we met. I had posted on Twitter and @ the salon. She replied and asked me if I liked my hair. We spoke on the phone, and she told me to come back to the shop so she could have it re-done the way I wanted. This time, it will be by a different stylist who she was sending me to that specialized in how I was getting my hair. The next day I went. After my hair was done I stayed around, and we talked for a few hours, got drinks and some food from Pearl, across the street from the shop. I had a bottle of my Mom's pills on me, she saw them and wanted to buy some. That's how we met and got cool.

I would visit the shop regularly to be serviced and see what she had going on. She was always asking somebody to stop by and see her and would have you there all day. I got close with the staff. It was like chilling in your home girl's living room. There was never a bad time. I lived on the complete opposite side of town, so most nights, after the salon would close, I'd ride with her and stay over to her house. That started turning into me staying for weeks at a time. I really didn't have too many friends in Atlanta besides Gizelle.

It wasn't like I worked a real job either and was busy during the day, so I would help her out. I was still figuring out what it was I wanted to do with myself. Though while being around her a couple of years, I was learning how to, I was also learning *how not* to run a business and *how not* to treat people. She was *really* manipulative of everybody she came in contact with and to keep it 100, was one of the best at what she was doing. She had a personality that would attract you to her but none of the friends she had stayed. There was always a motive behind what she was doing. It was only a hand full of people who were already hipped to the shit she did, and for me too, it took a minute before I took notice of it.

But the more I was around her, the more I noticed how she moved. I would wonder like *where the hell is this girl's family at? She's older, but why are all her friends people she just met or have only known a couple of years? Where are her friends from back in the day? She said she has brothers and sisters, where are they? Never even heard her on the phone with one. Where are her aunts, uncles, and even cousins? Why does nobody from her family deal with her? Never even seen her Mom stop by to wave at her.* The fact that I was around so much and never seen that. Now *that* was weird. But I still never worried too much about it though because I knew she wasn't crazy enough to pull anything on me. I didn't think twice.

I looked at her more of like a big sis because of our age difference.

I'd left Atlanta for a few months and went back to Ohio. I kept little contact with her, but when we'd speak, she would just keep saying she wasn't ok, to come see her and she'd tell me all about it. She didn't want to talk about it over the phone. I damn sure didn't think half the shit that was really going on. When I got back to the city, her house was one of my first stops. I wanted to check on her and see why she was saying all this. She was pregnant with her first child, told me she had just caught a new case, her baby's father was locked up, she was broke and shit at the salon was slow.

Once her baby's father was sent to prison shit for her got worse and worse for her. Eventually getting so far behind on her rent, she was being evicted. Her pride wouldn't let her tell me or anybody else that, so instead, she told us she was given a notice to leave the premises by the city of Atlanta because her landlord ran off with everybody's money "and the entire building was being foreclosed." But if that was the case, why did me and her need to ride all the way down to Alabama to meet bigcat for rent money she told him she needed? Story just wasn't adding up.

The sad part is she could have been telling the truth. It was just hard to believe, the way she'd lied about almost everything else and at this point was only trying to protect her reputation and the image she didn't want to lose. That still ended up being something she lost in the process because of all the bullshit and scamming she was doing to stay above water. Had people online placing orders for hair that she didn't even have and never sent out, then would block them on social media. Just doing people dirty. Stealing. Before it finally closed down, all the salon Staff were paid on commissions... she got 60%, they were supposed to get 40% and couldn't even get that.

She was "losing" their tickets with the services on it they did and paid them whatever she wanted to. The turnaround in there was a revolving door. She fell out with everybody who stood up for their self and made her pay them what they knew she owed them. It was embarrassing as hell. I put two and two together, *why did she ask me to do the payroll*, got everybody looking at me like I was crazy. Pissed at their $167 checks. She would fire them and say they were trying to get over on her.

Everybody was always lying if she told the story but I was seeing everything play out myself. What I was seeing her do to and say about so many people was tripping me out. She had the spirit of Jezebel. It was so much chaos, and I was seeing more of who she really was – scandalous. It was like she was doing whatever she could to make it look good. I guess I stayed a friend to her through it because I felt sorry for her situation and knew I was the last person she'd think about trying.

Even more so because since I had met her and considered her a friend of mine, I developed a true desire to see her succeed, like I did my other home girls. I wanted to see the vision she had for her business come to life. We talked about this type of shit daily. Our goals and executing each one. I think I cared more about her vision than she did some days.

That's how I was feeling. So when I saw she'd gotten to the point where she'd given up on it, I tried to contribute to turning that around. The ones I'd say were her *real friends*; I could tell, felt the same way. Everybody was trying to help. Those were the ones she talked down on and dogged the most. Then dick-ride whoever she knew was poppin' at the time or that had a following but could clearly care less about her. Just to keep a *friend's* name, she could drop when she needed to.

She was good at that – name dropping. She did so much talking about her relationship with Meech that he never acknowledges and had ended over a decade ago, her *family ties* to BMF, the very first day I met her. You would've never thought her real man was sitting at home. You don't even have to bring it up or ask; it's just like an affiliation she *desperately wants* you to know she had. She's the one that's going to tag you in a post every chance given unnecessarily. Her method was to befriend those who she thought had a little buzz or already had a name for themselves, kiss their ass and keep them as close as possible to be able to sound or look connected.

Whether she liked you or not, the reality that her time had come and gone years ago wasn't registering, and the girl was having a hard time dealing with that. It worked. People would listen to what she had to say once she had them thinking she was the one with the answers. She was smart enough and had a mouthpiece on her like any other manipulative person you're going to meet. When combining the two, in today's world, you can create influence amongst *anybody* that doesn't know you well enough.

The masses normally are fooled first. So like I said, it worked. She had a lot of people fooled thinking she was somebody to fear. Hunnie I was just trying to figure out where all these *riders* were when she had a mailbox full of disconnection notices and food stamp sanctions. I didn't see the loyalty from any of the people she would say was her family and squad. Not even on the backend, *my real people are a secret* side. They didn't exist. But I *was* there to see consistent love and support from the same people she tried to convince me and others weren't shit and to look down on. They meant nothing to her. Can't forget about that vanishing salon staff that she'd robbed blind every payroll. Oh, they were *all liars, clout chasing lames and beneath her*. I didn't miss *any* of that.

January 21, 2013. What led up to this? Like usual, I'd been back and forth almost every day from my house to hers, this time for about two or three weeks. Her son was now five months old, baby father was still in prison, and she had been in this house suffering from a whole lot of postpartum depression breakdown situation, was broke, miserable and struggling bad. Just really dealing with the karma that had caught up with her.

This day she had asked me to go with her to the ER, her son was really sick. We'd been there all day. When we pulled up to her house, I told her I was about to drive to the nail shop. She grabbed her baby out from the backseat of her car, and I left. I'd told her I was going to the one near her house, but once I got there, it was closed. Of course, I didn't think to call and tell her that I was going to a different one. Two years of living in ATL, I still didn't really know my way everywhere, so I relied on my GPS to take me to the next nearest nail shop that was open. The closest one was Atlantic Station. I was able to get my nails done then stopped next door to Yardhouse to get something to eat.

I ordered my food then texted her to see if she wanted anything. She never text back then called yelling on top of her lungs. Talking crazy! *Where the fuck are you at with my car bitch didn't nobody tell you to go all the way to Atlantic Station to do all that!* I thought like she *had* to be playing. Ain't no way in hell this bitch is talking to me like that. She had me fucked up the first five seconds of the call I was pissed!

As soon as I started talking, she hung up. She called back with K. Michelle on three-way. I was confused on what that was even supposed to mean. Like was I supposed to give a fuck? Was this her way of "ganging up" to check me? Who did she think she was playing sweet? Come on baby; you're 34 years old doing three-way calls. Are you serious? I didn't even know her home girl like that. We had only just met a few weeks before then and had all been around each other a few times. Not to mention how bad she was just talking about this woman, her career and personal business she *thought I cared to hear about.*

All I could think was you *got the right one. I ain't none of them girls you had in your shop getting over on or lames you got trying to be your friend. I'll get out here and get with you real quick. I ain't done shit to you but tried to help you bitch. You could never be that mad over a trip to the nail shop. I've never a day in my life fought a friend but you sound like you don't see this going any other way. What's up?* She yelled in the phone *Bitch! Get here right the fuck now and make sure my gas tank is where I had it!* I just know damn well this ain't about you being worried you wouldn't have gas.

I told her I was about to bring her that dumb ass car and she could take it anywhere she wanted it to go. I had the intention of filling *up* her tank until she called. I had never driven her car before and didn't. I knew she didn't have it. I did not know where this was all coming from. I was lost! Just ready to get there to see what she was talking about. Me being me, I took my time, stopped at the BP right on Glenwood around the corner from her house. Passed the pumps, went inside and bought a lighter. Smoked and drove to her house. I didn't know that once I pulled into the driveway, it was about to turn life or death for me.

I pulled back into her driveway, turned off the engine and opened the car door. I was reaching in the backseat for my purse when I heard the back door slam and heard her voice, still yelling! *Here's yo shit! Get yo ass out my car!* She had my stuff packed into the bag I brought it over in to come help her with her sick son. The nerve of this bitch.

Back the fuck up! She was so close up on me at the car door that I couldn't move from where I was and how I was sitting. We were definitely about to fight, which is cool, but she was going to let me up out that car first. I looked over, and she was swinging fast but opened handed. She was clearly never trying to punch me; she had other plans. With every swing, she was slicing me up with a box cutter she had in her hand that I didn't see. I didn't know. Here I am swinging back with a closed fist. I'd been fighting all my life; I wasn't worried about a scuffle. I was still thinking it was a regular street fight and not an attack from somebody who was scared to fight. All the shit she talked I knew for sure she was ready to box.

She screamed *Stop! Stop! You're bleeding! Stop!* I saw blood running down my arms. She had cut me up! With a razor! I didn't see it in her hand until she backed up. My neck and hands felt like a match had been lit on them! I couldn't believe it.

I thought she would never try me, but she did and went all out with it, in a Snapped, Lifetime movie style. I got out the car so I could stand up. Tried to take her head off! She ran into the house, snatched her baby off the couch, ran back out to her car that door was still open to and sped off. She was still yelling out her window while taking off down the street but I couldn't hear her. I was having a panic attack from all the blood I was looking at all over my clothes. On her back porch, it was blood puddles over the pavement. It wasn't until she had pulled off that I realized I was fucked up like that. I didn't know *where* all this warm blood was coming from!

I looked down at my leg and saw a gash as big as my hand and almost passed out! Any time I talk about this night, I can hear the sound of my own voice, crying and screaming begging them to hurry up and get to me. You could hear the fear in my voice. I really thought I was going to die in that backyard. She left me there to die. She had no idea how bad she had cut me. She just saw blood and left.

What happened? Too close to the wrong people. The devil. A snake can only be what it is – a snake. Who you are to them doesn't matter. They're everywhere in every circle. I'm sure it's a lot harder being them than it is dealing with them, but knowing *how* to handle a snake is what's most important. I learned a lot from that night. From that situation period. People will try their best to hide behind Bible scriptures and lies but at the end of the day, a person can only truly be who they are, and they can't hide from that. What they'll do to somebody else they'll do to you, and it's a reason for everything.

She called first, crying and basically saying that everything she was going through had made her snap and she was out of her mind right now. Saying how sorry she was and scared because of her probation and if she went to prison, she didn't have anybody to take care of her son. It was a whole dramatic act, and she was full of shit. Then spent the next week trying to have people reach out to me. Doing whatever, begging whoever she could to get help with the money she tried to offer for cutting me but that's not what I wanted. Some of the calls I got were from people I knew for sure she hated. That's how I knew she was desperate. *Every day* there was somebody else on my phone she asked to call or text me.

She was the one who had stabbed *me,* and after however her P.O. got involved, was now playing a police game so serious that I didn't know *what* was going on. My friend Kevin was murdered days before this happened and I had to rush out to Ohio to go to his funeral. I left Atlanta.

The next and last time I saw her was when I got subpoenaed to court. Dekalb County had picked it up and charged her with Aggravated Assault. She came with her attorney who played a 911 call in the courtroom that was supposed to be me but was saying things I know I never said. Til' this day that shit still creeps me out. They pressed play and the first 60 seconds of the call was muted. Coincidentally the most important part of the call wasn't playing, and they didn't have an answer why. You could hear me screaming crying and yelling when the dispatcher was asking for the location.

Then in a deep voice that wasn't mine, you hear "I'm going to kill your baby!" I was looking at that man like he was crazy. They knew damn well that wasn't me! I don't know *how* her attorney did it, but from then on, that was the story she stuck to and told publicly. That and in court, said I was trying to extort her out of money. She had printed out fake text messages, but that made her look dumb because the messages that were supposed to be from *me* were coming from the wrong bubble. My posts on Twitter were printed out, and her attorney brought those to court too. The picture she was trying to paint of me was just sad. Neither of the two made sense!

First of all, she didn't have anything to extort her out of and the fact that the ambulance was called because I was stabbed, was obviously because *I had already been cut!* Her story was, she cut me *because* "I said that I was going to kill her baby." Now how could that even be possible for me to already be on the phone getting help when in the call that was played in court, you can hear a voice say *"I'm going to kill your baby."*

If that was really "why she cut me," that would've had to have been something I'd done *before* the ambulance was called. *Whatever caused me to get cut, happened before the ambulance was called for help... which was after I was cut up.* I never once spoke out or spoke up about what happened when it hit all the blogs, and people in Atlanta were talking about it.

I just sat back and let her tell her story and watched how it twisted, turned and never made any sense. I never pressed charges against her and never went to another court hearing. She got sentenced to six punk ass months in prison, but that was only for violating her probation that she was already on, and did the other six months in an Atlanta halfway house.

I'm more scared of scared people than I am of anything else because those are the ones that'll do whatever. They talk all day about what they'll do and about how tough and hard they are, but when it's time to pull up, they're never there. If they are, even when they know you're coming empty handed, they're bringing a weapon. Scared to death! That's a dangerous situation to be in. All the getting over on people she had done over the years, she never knew what was coming which way or from who.

People needing to avoid coming in contact with certain people, they take precautions and don't come outside. There isn't enough voodoo dolls in this world that weird ass bitch can play with. Not enough of those potions she kept in spell alters, or candles she burned on people that could have me worried about anything. Sabrina and everything she represents is a big ass joke that only people on an App could take serious.

That's it.

Chapter 7

FREE AT LAST

I'd flown out to Los Angeles to visit my family and get some work done. I was enjoying the hell out of that warm California weather in March. I was in the streets moving around every day. Out at the beach, everywhere, talking to new people. My main focus for coming all the way West was to grow my brand out there in a new market, so I was doing a lot of footwork. Setting up events and getting myself out there. I was going so hard, every single day. That's all I would do was work. My business was blowing up fast. My dedication and consistency was paying off.

It became all that I was worried about. I was determined for this to work for me, and I was serious about helping as many people as I could do the same thing and it worked too! I was growing professionally, my income was growing, hair was growing, skin was glowing. I had never made that much money before or had money like that moving through my account monthly, and neither had anybody else where I came from unless it was tax season. This was a real good feeling for me because after all I'd just gone through and all the other small things I'd tried to do before, that didn't work, I'd finally found my lane, and it was changing my life.

Driving down the 104 freeway my phone rang. It was LaDarius! *Meagan where you at?* I knew exactly who it was when I heard that voice and damn was I happy to hear it again. We kept it short, but I knew what that call meant. GET HERE! I must have changed departure dates so quick! He's home! He was out! I left California and flew into Ohio. As soon as I got in the city, I called him back.

That night we met up with each other and got a room. We had so much to talk about and catch up on. I hadn't seen him and barely spoke to him his whole bid. I don't think it really had dawned on me just how much I'd missed being with him. Even without the sex and all the extra shit, me and LA could kick it with each other and not want to leave from around each other for days. We really were *friends first*. That was a real good night. He said *I see you learned some new tricks living in Atlanta. I don't even want to know! I like it though.*

It was only a couple of weeks that had gone by before I had found a new apartment in Columbus. We were spending way too much money at these rooms, and neither one of us wanted to spend a night away from each other, so I didn't waste no time getting a place for us to live together. I still had my apartment in Atlanta when I did this. Mind you; originally I'd left on vacation to Cali and never made it back once LA got out of prison. I didn't go back home after that. I remember calling my leasing office in Atlanta and asking them to take the food out of my refrigerator so that it wouldn't be *walking* by the time I made it back.

I wasn't *where* I wanted to be, but I'm with *who* I wanted to be with. As long as I was with him nothing else mattered. What I *really* wanted was for him to come to Atlanta with me and live, but he didn't feel right doing that without getting himself together first, so Ohio is where we stayed. I went and found us a nice two bedroom place in Canal Winchester that was also a new build. When we moved in, I did everything I could to make this "home" for the both of us. Especially for my man. I wanted our home to be that guaranteed place of peace for him.

Somewhere away from the loud, busy neighborhood that he spent his days in. Our apartment was real quiet and comfortable if it wasn't anything else. I feel like where ever you lay your head should be like that. I always would keep it clean. Me and Beth. Our cleaning lady. She would come for me on Tuesdays, but through the week I was washing his clothes, keeping the house straight, and cooking. I didn't even know *how* to cook! I'm the baby of my family, the youngest of my friends, so I've always been the one who's gotten catered to and cooked for. I tried to learn quick how to be that for LaDarius. It was funny! I didn't know what the hell I was doing; I was just doing it!

LA must have lost 100lbs from living with me. That was love in itself the way he stuck around through my brown eggs and dry, overcooked fish. I was trying! I would burn my sage in an attempt to keep the bad spirits and bad energy out that I felt may have followed him from being out there. I kept fresh flowers and candles going. It was a whole vibe, at all times. The whole nine. My goal has always been for my home to feel somewhere between a resort/hotel and worry-free "homie home," like your Grandma's house would be. Somewhere you can't wait for your day to end so that you can get back to. That's what I did.

I was proud of what I made our first place together out to be. It was a nice thing to leave behind those bars and come home to. This was my first time living with a man full time; I got in the role. I just wanted him to *love being home* so that just maybe he'd *hate being in the streets*. In a way, that kind of worked too. His homeboys would say shit like *Damn! Do you ever leave from under her? All you wanna do is be under your girl's ass. Damn you allowed out tonight?* I wasn't keeping him from them, and I never forced LA to do anything.

He wasn't like that with me either. We had the choice to be wherever we wanted to be but chose to be with each other most of the time. If you see a couple that's like this and who're in love or just enjoying each other, respect it. Nothing is wrong with that. We have to stop making it an issue or something negative. For men, it doesn't make you soft to be in a relationship and be loyal to your woman. It's not lame to spend time with your girl and family. Especially amongst the black community, we don't see this often. So we have to stop down talking it. It brainwashes young boys.

Next thing you know they don't like girls anymore because they've trained their self to hate and disrespect females their whole life... then they become the trade. Some guys get too worried about looking like a sucker to their homies, that they never allow themselves to get too deep into their relationship and lose it or end up never having a real one. That's a lost man. I think more of what it was for LA is that he *always put me first*. If you weren't with us, you were against us, and that's a fact. Even when I was wrong, I was right. Everybody couldn't handle it. If you've never been on either end of a relationship like that, you won't respect it. It didn't stop us or slow us down though.

We would go out all the time. Me and LA... Tyk, Hell Rell, Fat Mack and Mario. Mario had also just gotten out of prison too. He had been there since he was a juvenile, him and LA ran together back in the day and ended up being released weeks apart. It would be us, them and a whole slew of other guys from the Southside walking in clubs and bars that whole summer. You couldn't miss them. Monday through Sunday we were out. I would run my business during the day, get done with everything, maybe have a meeting, do some conference calls, then be out the rest of the night with him.

I don't recall really seeing too much of any other side of town out in 2013. Some didn't bother to show their faces knowing certain guys could walk through the door at any time. Then you had some who enjoyed the back and forth confrontation and the conflict, so they came out anyway. This is when the big bar fights would happen. By then I felt like I'd already had my days and was trying to put all that behind me. I hated it. I went from being that girl who'd avoid even coming into contact with these guys, to being there *with* these troublesome ass niggas.

It was crazy. We had fun, but I think I spent more time watching our surroundings than I did getting drifted off with everybody else. I would be staring at niggas, stare at LA. I watched their body language, movements, and mouths. There were things I knew LA or somebody else with us had done to people in the past and things I had no idea they were still out here doing, that kept me alert like that when we got around crowds. Everybody had guns! That's just the type of city Columbus is. Homicide rates in the hundreds, every year.

You can only imagine the anxiety being in settings like that. It didn't matter where we went, that's just the energy that followed this group. There was *a lot* of money blown doing this. When I finally looked at the statements, close to half of what I was making was going to partying. All you need to do is not pay attention, and spending $600 a week will happen quick.

Like most black men who were in the streets before, gone to prison and come home, it wasn't taking long at all before LaDarius began slowly drifting out of my hands. It was becoming a problem. I just couldn't understand why he always needed to be everywhere, all the time. He could only sit in the same place for so long, like he was going to miss something. I wanted him *home* like he'd *been* doing, but his argument was *how do you expect me to be able to make anything happen, or get anything done sitting in this house all day?*

As if there weren't any other options, he was running out of patience. Sick and tired of waiting. I wanted him to go to work, pay our bills and let me flip the income I had, so we wouldn't have to do anything we didn't want to. I wanted him to give me one year, and I was going to retire him from that job. That's not even something he was considering. He was getting pissed. His own homies was scared to fuck with him. Didn't want to serve or shop with him. Everybody looked at him like a grimy ass nigga you couldn't completely trust.

They were dying in my city every other day about stuff like that. But that's really not what he was on. It's a bad feeling being a man and *wanting* to take care of your family but not being able to, because of a reputation you've already built. Regardless of him seeing the route I was taking, he still resorted right back to the neighborhood to figure it out. It didn't matter what he saw me get, how much he saw me count or what he knew I had on the way, LA would *never, ever* ask me for anything and gave me whatever he got.

Normally you'd hear about guys coming home from prison, and their girl hands them start-ups. He wouldn't allow me to even if that was me. But it's not. I love hard, yes, but I don't believe in glass houses. I'd rather you build something that's solid and stable. I wasn't being handed anything, and I'm not one to hand anything to anyone I want to see do better for themselves. Everything LA had I wanted him to work hard for so he could appreciate it. He didn't want any help either. From anybody. He's a protector and provider in every sense of the word. He wanted desperately to take care of me. He did whatever he needed to, to make sure it happened too. Nobody was safe.

Chapter 8

STILL GOIN' IN

Since the day LA came home, he had a new situation that I knew almost more than anything, stressed him out and fueled the angry, frustrated madman I had to deal with. Baby mama drama! He wasn't used to all this. He'd never been anybody's baby's father. This was all damn near cultural shock. I'm talking about, straight out the prison cell she gave him hell. He had a whole Dashiki situation going on with this girl. He didn't know what he had gotten himself into. Loud, ratchet, ignorant... couldn't put together a literate sentence but would start texting and calling his phone at 7 am looking for a problem.

You could tell whatever happened to her, at whatever point in her life that it left her damaged, miserable and bitter. Just a mess. This was that. But that's what *niggas* do right? They'll leave their home, nice ones too - To go sneak and freak at a hoe's filthy house, on her mattress that doesn't have sheets on it, sitting on the floor somewhere. Good women go through this at some point. Where we look at *who* he did it with, and it makes us look at ourselves like *Damn! Am I this nigga's type?* This baby mama was a day to day pest who didn't have nothing going on for herself. I want to say the very first time we went over her house to pick his son up; I sat in the car.

She opened the door to hand the baby to him and yelled out *I know you ain't bring this bitch to my house!* I was so mad lol. I had got out the car and everything, Mario pulled me back in, and it wasn't about nothing. Note you, I had never been introduced to her, never heard anything about her. Didn't know who she was. Had no problem with her *at all. I thought*. She did all this just off the strength that *LA was her bae dad*. Till this day, I don't know what LA had promised that girl before he got out of prison, or what they'd done before I got to Ohio to see him, but seeing us together was fucking her up.

It was beef! That's what most of our arguments were about – females. He started creeping around with different girls, and our relationship just got weird. He wasn't ashamed of it, and it was about to cost him everything he had with me. Exactly what I meant when I said guys would try to make their homeboys feel lame if they aren't out here doing whatever they want. When a man is in a relationship but kicks it with his nothing ass friends who all cheat on their girls, then that's the route he's more than likely going to take too. LA thought he could do whatever he wanted, so that's what he did.

It was females everywhere! But for whatever reason, this one, in particular, was so jealous and envious of what me and LA had going on. She constantly went out of her way to do extra shit, or would stay on his line harassing him about something that fake had to do with their son. If she could get me mad at him or could get him mad at me, she was all for it. In her mind, what we had was what she wanted *them* to have. She put up her best fight to try and make that happen, sometimes that meant fighting me.

After our second run in, I didn't have to worry about her trying me again, but I was just sick of the drama. She didn't plan on going away even with every effort put forth being a failed attempt. To the social media and to LA's family, she first had to make me out to be the bad guy. I got accused of dogging her son at least once a week. Of course, anybody would jump to defend a baby, but that's the oldest trick in the book. It's the easiest thing you can accuse someone of doing without giving facts. She was never able to be specific about anything I supposedly said, but nobody ever asked either.

I'd had enough! When LaDarius would bring his son to our house, I'd love up on him as if he was my own. He never got treated like a stepchild. If it was something his Dad couldn't do, I picked up. Christmas, Birthday, diapers, shoes, clothes. We never would bother making it clear who it came from; we would just get it done. I really loved that baby. By nature, I'm this type of woman. I've raised my two nephews since they came home from the hospital. Like really *raised*. So it was nothing to me making sure a child that's at my house is well kept. I knew more about how to be a parent than he did.

I was only helping him do his part. I accepted everything that came with this man, his child too. I wasn't resentful towards him for it because it's not like we were together when this happened, I was barely taking him serious before he went to prison. To me, it didn't have to be a problem like people may have thought it was. I was ok with it; I was dealing with a babymama that was worsome though.

So it was never that simple. I felt bad he was being used as a pawn, because I always knew in my heart that he was not LA's son, for a fact. They shared none of the same features. The Meeks have strong genes. You know those families where if you're kin to them it's all in your face... that's a Meeks. They all look the same. He just didn't have that.

You couldn't have paid me to send my child off with their Dad and his girl who I can't stand, looking the way she would send him with us. LA would be so mad! If I'm going to give you something to talk about, it won't be my skills as a Mother. I wouldn't talk down on her son because not only is that just not me, but I mean, what really is there *bad* to say about a *baby*? I would talk about what she was doing. What I saw, and it was all facts. These were still the conversations me and LA kept between us.

He may say something to his Mom about it, but that was it. I was never ignorant the way this girl was about anything; I dealt with whatever came to me and left it at that. I did what I could to make this child a part of his life, but I never let up on what I felt. Something wasn't adding up, and I wanted to see some DNA, especially now! Like girl, you're harassing us over whatever you can, whenever you can. Would have LA begging to see and get his son all because he has a girl and it's not you.

The shit started getting old, and LaDarius was tired of crying over her games. Yeah, let me do us all a favor and get you on out the way. I don't like anything that brings the worst out of me, and that's what had been going on. I was tired of this being in my space, for no reason. Had she not been the way she was, I probably would have never even pressed the issue but something had to shake before this got any more out of control.

LA kept promising me he would do it, but months went by, and it wasn't getting done. I started threatening to leave him over those tests, that's how over it I was! She was furious any time I brought it up. Even more so once LA and I found out we were pregnant! Damn. Finally, a family of our own.

We had tried and tried for what seemed like forever to have a baby together. I remember around when we first started talking; he would tell me *I'm going to make you my wife and have my kids with you.* He had no idea that being somebody's wife and pushing out a baby was the last things on my list when we met. It wasn't even a thought. I was young and living my best life.

I'm not the Oh I like him, or we're in love, now let's have a baby type. That's something serious to me. This pregnancy was for sure planned mostly by LA. I just agreed. LA would not get off my back about us getting pregnant, or should I say wouldn't let me off my back! Oh my God! He wanted this more than anything in the world. I could care less about sex until we start living together. I loved making love to him. I guess that's where Hiyah came from.

I got sick with meningitis and was admitted to the hospital for a week. That's when the doctors told us we were pregnant. LA was on his way back up there to bring me something to eat. Chipotle is what I asked him for, but being LA, he bought me food from some new place downtown that he swore was so much better. Man, he brought that food to the door of my room, and I yelled for him not to come any closer with that shit! It was making me nauseated before he even made it in! It was the smell of the meat.

My Mom told him to come on anyway, and she would eat it if I didn't, he did what she told him to do, and I was so mad! That throw up was shooting out of my mouth like I had acid reflux. My Mom turned to LaDarius, *Oh hell no! She's pregnant! She's pregnant ain't no way the smell of this is gonna have you throwing up. You can barely smell it!* I don't think I said anything until she left. Even though he already knew about it, we hadn't gotten a chance to talk about it yet because my Mom got there so fast. I was going to tell her, but me and LA needed this moment to ourselves. No sooner than my Mom walked out of the room, LA looked at me and smiled harder than he did that day outside the store when he saw me again. *I love you so much baby! Thank you so much for doing this Meagan! I promise I got y'all.* I told him not to tell anybody yet; I had a plan on the way we would let everybody know.

This boy left straight out the hospital doors and told *everybody*! He might have told the strangers he passed on his way through the Lobby. He didn't listen. His Aunt called me while I was still in my room, in the bed. I was pregnant, and they all knew. LA was so excited; the man couldn't keep his mouth shut. Nervous and all, I was just as happy as he was.

Chapter 9

PARALYZED TO THE STREETS

"So Many Tears." A song by my favorite person ever created. Tupac. I feel like he spoke for so many of us. Specifically, those who feel like their lives are similar to the title of this chapter.

"Now I'm lost and I'm weary, so many tears

I'm suicidal so don't stand near me

My every move is a calculated step

To bring me closer to embrace an early death

Now there's nothin' left

There was no mercy on the streets

I couldn't rest, I'm barely standin'

About to go to pieces, screamin' peace

And though my soul was deleted, I couldn't see it

In my mind full of demons tryna break free

They planted seeds and they hatched, sparkin' the flame

Married To The Bad Guy

Inside my brain like a match, such a dirty game

No memories, just a misery

Paintin' a picture of my enemies killin' me in my sleep

Will I survive til the mornin' to see the sun?

Please Lord, forgive me for my sins, cause here I come

He went on to say...

And Lord knows I tried, **been a witness to homicide**

Seen drive-by's takin' lives, little kids die

Wonder why as I walk by

Broken-hearted as I glance at the chalk line, gettin' high

This ain't the life for me, I wanna change

But ain't no future bright for me, I'm stuck in the game

I'm trapped inside a maze

See this Tanqueray influenced me to gettin' crazy

Disillusioned lately, **I've been really wantin' babies**

So I could see a part of me that wasn't always shady

Don't trust my lady, cause she's a product of this poison

I'm hearin' noises, think she's fuckin all my boys

Can't take no more, I'm fallin to the floor

Beggin' for the Lord to let me in to Heaven's door

Shed so many tears."

Me and LaDarius were more friends than we were anything else, and as his girl, I obviously wanted nothing but the best for both of us. I introduced him to anything he didn't know about, that I did. After we moved in together, a lot about him changed, people noticed it and would tell him. Everything from the stores he shopped at to the types of meals he ate. He watched me run my business daily and build a brand from nothing, so he was learning the ins and outs of what that really looks like and took his own notes.

Anything I learned, I shared with him. I would have him read the books I had in the house, coming with me to my meetings. I would ask him for his input before I made decisions, he would sit up with me at night, drink glasses of wine and strategize. I wanted him to see firsthand, anything he had dreams of doing, he could – we *could*. For the first time ever, he told me what he wanted out of life. He shared his dreams with me. Told me his plan.

A couple of days after I bought my dream car, we jumped on the road. It was brand new. We drove to D.C. for my training. We stayed extra days and had a ball together. That was my first time leaving the state with him. To see him enjoying himself and hearing him tell his friends and family about the places we would travel to, was a good feeling. All I wanted was to give him *experiences* that I knew for sure he would never get on Oakwood or 22nd. I did things with LA that I knew he wouldn't forget. I thought if I could expose him to more, it would broaden his horizons and motivate him to want more for himself than settling for what he was getting. His mindset would change. I did that from day one.

You rarely saw LA and didn't see me. We had built a life together both giving each other something we didn't have. I loved to wake up, and this man's handsome face was the first thing I see in the morning. Our daughter was on the way, and he didn't feel right bringing her into this world without first making some things forever.

On the morning of... LaDarius woke me up; I couldn't forget the look in his eyes if I wanted to. I didn't know what was different about how he was acting, but I could feel it all over. Like this was something he thought about a long time. Later on, he told me he never went to sleep that night. He said he stayed up watching me sleep. *"I wouldn't know what to do for the rest of my life with anybody else but you. I waited on you I don't want to do this with nobody else."* We had stayed up from probably 11 pm to 4 am, and as soon as I fall asleep, this is how he woke me. *"Let's get Meagan. Please, I got you. Will you?"* I sat up, naked in our bed and held his face in my hands; I couldn't stop crying. I was not expecting that.

The tingling feelings that rush through your chest, hands, and legs when you're walking up to speak in front of a room full of strangers is how I was feeling. I didn't know what to say. *For real Darius!?* I don't know if it was the sound of my voice mixed with the thoughts rushing through his head or what, but he just stared at me and started to cry too. *"I love you so much Meagan. I promise not to let you down or mess this up."* Yes, I will. I love you too baby. *"Let's go to the courthouse. What do we need to do? We can have the wedding however you want to once Hiyah gets here. I don't want you to have her without being my Wife."*

Meagan Alexander. I gave him exactly what he asked me for. We decided to do this by ourselves, so we prayed in the car and went downtown alone. Even though marriage was nothing I'd ever thought about, it made sense. That's what he was supposed to do. I was excited! We had barely left the building, and I was uploading pictures to social media. In seconds our phones were ringing back to back. My timeline flooded in congratulating posts, and of course, the screenshots began! Our friends couldn't believe it and neither could our families. LaDarius was so proud. That was November 5th, 2013.

Me and this man have one of the most, if *not* the most controversial, non-traditional relationships. I feel like considering how intentionally private I am with my personal life and my marriage, that there's still no secrets we can keep. No privacy. Every move, somebody, somewhere, wants to know how and why it was made. A lot of people in Columbus know the both of us, but we're known for completely different things. For us to do what we did together, wasn't what anybody would've expected. One thing we didn't need any more of was attention.

We were followed closely by different people for different reasons, but we were both targets. LA had done so much bullshit to people that he was someone they wanted out the way. With me, any time you're doing the right thing around the wrong people, you'll be a target. Don't believe me? Just start looking like you might just make it to the same people who saw you struggle and you'll learn quick that they were way more comfortable and liked you better when they could compare and relate to you.

There will be hate. It comes with the territory. Then I would think maybe people make shit such a big deal all the time because I always make shit a big deal? I don't know, but they sure talked about it. There was a lot of gossip. A lot of stories. Some were happy for us, some mad. None of which truly mattered, we just did us. I spent the next couple of months planning a whole new life. I had my Husband and a baby on the way. Working from home, I had nothing *but time*. Came up with locations, lists, dresses, color themes. Hiyah's Sip & See, delivery day and did a bunch of shopping for her. I kept myself busy.

It seemed like as soon as we got married, trouble found us. I didn't have to go looking for it; I didn't have to start it. It just came. Most of the people close to us that were team LA & Meagan before, hated us now. It was always something to say. Me and LA's Dad fell out first. People would make jokes and say every time I walk in the room Mr. Alexander's face lit up. They'd say "that man likes you." I never thought about it like that because I thought what we had was a daughter-father bond, but once we got married, I started noticing the weird stuff.

He would get upset if I wouldn't answer his phone calls or wouldn't come see him. One night LA needed to get something from his Mom, and we went over there. I had to use the bathroom, so I came in too. I walked in, and his sister told me their Dad did not like me anymore and said I wasn't allowed in. Mr. Alexander came down the stairs furious and told me to get out of his house! Real nasty too. I was confused as hell. I literally had done *nothing* at all to this God-fearing Pastor! Yet, he was still kicking his pregnant daughter in law out of his apartment.

LA was more mad than I was because *knew* what was up. Him and his Dad had some words, but we left. It wasn't until almost a year later that me, LA, his Mom and Mr. Alexander all sat down in their living room to talk, did his Dad say the reason he stopped talking to me was that "I let LA take me away from HIM when LA got out of jail." He went on to say I was acting funny towards him and would dodge him. Here I am thinking he was about to say he felt like I had taken his son away from him and he was talking about me! Creepy! Me and LA must have looked at each other like *what the fuck did he say?* The sad part is by then, he had already manipulated the whole family into thinking I was a bad person and had done him some type of wrong. His Mom was the only person I talked to. She was always so sweet and positive. She never got herself into the middle of anything regardless of who was doing what. Nobody in his family who didn't like me even knew why they didn't anymore; they just didn't. When the last time I'd seen them, it was all laughs and smiles.

They couldn't tell you why or would have a reason today if you asked. I don't know what he could have even been telling them or if they were just bored, but that was the weirdest shit! LA hated how nobody got along. Although he didn't want to seem like, to anybody that he was taking sides, he *never* went against me. We were together day in and day out, so he already knew I hadn't done shit. LA was fighting for me right or wrong. In *any* situation... as he should. But everybody didn't want to respect that. I did the same for him with my family.

If you were against him, you were against me. When my Mom and GiGi called their self not liking my Husband, I stayed away too. We come as one. I looked at it as I wish this wasn't how things were, but all we really need is each other when this is all said and done. We were both ok with that. Had someone like me been there the way that I've been there for LA, for one of my brothers, cousins or nephews and was actually somebody who I could clearly see was bringing the best out of him and that person is who makes him happy, I would have never! LaDarius would tell me all the time I saved his life by coming in it. The first time he told me that, I didn't understand what he meant. But it didn't take long before I did.

To me, he was still too accessible. Any time people are able to reach you with one phone call and can get to you whenever they want to, by pulling up to a certain spot, you're too accessible. Whenever you're living like this, you shouldn't be easy to get a hold of like that. When you are, you're easy to get rid of too. I didn't trust anybody. Nothing I did, or we did together was keeping him 100% on the right track. Like my Mom, he couldn't shake it. I'm humble enough to say I will always love the hood too, but I *never* want to be stuck there mentally or physically. I'm never settling.

You're supposed to live and succeed out to be able to *remember when*. I'm not giving my all to a place that's only ever taken from me. A lot of his best memories and funnest times were on deuce, some of mine were too. But a lot of his worst memories and times were made in the same place.

When we could no longer tell who the snakes were, I did everything I could to make sure they didn't trick mine off the streets. I would tell LA if they weren't his blood, cut it out. There were a lot of yes men who only wanted to be around him, Mario and Tyk for protection. I was watching it. These niggas didn't even want to go outside if they weren't coming with them. Like, it had just started to get way too obvious.

So when we'd be in the house and at 12, 1 am, his phone would ring, and it was somebody asking him to meet them somewhere *that's* when I would tell him he wasn't going anywhere. There were times he listened, other times he still got up and walked out the door.

I think I developed this bad anxiety that I deal with, from years of long nights, staying up waiting for him to come home. Actually making it "in" safely, in one whole piece was a blessing, I saw it as another chance. The 10tv news app I had on my phone wouldn't do anything but stress me out. Notifications would flash across my screen and be titled "One dead, one in critical condition in Eastside shooting" and I'd start blowing his phone up. I never wanted to see his name on the news as someone who something happened to or the person who'd done something to somebody else. I was literally praying that I see his face again at the end of the day – every day.

There is absolutely *no peace* in being scared to pull off from places like grocery stores and gas stations always, wondering if the car behind you is following you or that car beside you at a red light is somebody your man has problem with, who'll take your life or kidnap *you to get back at him*. I feared retaliation. These were the things I'd think about on days that nothing was wrong. *We could walk out our front door right now and not make it to the car.* When friends were setting up friends, I knew the loyalty in the neighborhood was lost, and anything could happen at any time. I took out a life insurance policy on LA in 2013, and we had his lawyer create and notarize a document making me his power of attorney.

You'd had thought with everything we had going on, that Meagan and LA were as happy as it got, but to say the least, we weren't. People are easily misled thinking because they'll never leave someone that they will ever be happy, or that love itself is enough to force two people together forever; it's not. Outsiders could never come between us, but the streets did. I thought that if he was man enough to pass me his last name and make me somebody's Mom, he'd better be, should be, man enough to stay out of the way of anything that could prevent this. He didn't. Here we were again, back to square one, them or us?

Chapter 10

CAN'T RAISE A MAN

One thing you can't do, I don't care how hard you try, this isn't up for debate, is raise a man. You just can't. There are certain things they have instilled in them as children and choices they have to make themselves as adults that nobody else is involved in, that will calculate how they move. Depending on when you got to them, you don't know what the hell he's been through, what hell he's been through or what type of females he's used to being with. You don't know what he's used to getting away with. How he's used to living.

You don't know who hurt him in the past or how it changed the way he deals with women. You're just figuring it out as you go. As time passes, you can encourage him to do things differently, you can show him different, you can even threaten him of what you'll do if he does or doesn't do something in specific.

But you can't *make* a grown man be who you want him to be. People do what they're ready to do on their own time. Nine times out of ten, they already are who they're going to be. Trying to change them, will only change *you* in the process. That's what I found myself doing with LA. Trying to push him into being the person I'd convinced myself he had the potential to be. As women, we sometimes, for years, get stuck on who we *know* our man *could be* if he only would stop or start doing this or that. *STOP*

HANGING ON TO POTENTIAL!

What I learned through that was it's a hit or miss. In my experiences, it's been more misses than hits, and if it turned out to be a hit, I went through hell to get there. It damned sure wasn't until *after* I walked away from the situation and if you're anything like me, once I'm done, I'm the fuck done! Ain't no coming back. I don't give a fuck who you are.

LA was struggling between living two completely different lifestyles being with me. Even though I knew he loved *us*, I also knew he loves being who he'd *been* too. He kept running into problems trying to do that because I've always demanded more from him than he was used to giving.

It was almost like he was fighting the new him with the old him every day. It was frustrating the hell out of him. He stopped being able to hide how frustrated he was anymore, and he acted on it. His attitude got so shitty – up and down. He was never the same man waking up, that he was going to sleep. You didn't know what you were going to get day to day. LaDarius or LA. He was just stuck in his ways. He was loyal to all the wrong people and was a product of his environment. I was to a point then where I'd had all the dealings with the streets and street niggas that I wanted.

I was waking up every day, building my business, working hard to do things differently with my life than what I always had and what I'd always had around me. The shit he was doing didn't suit me anymore. I wasn't impressed, I was angry. When I was younger and wilder, yeah it was cool. When I was 13, 14, 15yrs old, it was cool to me to kick it in the hood with the homies when I got off work, sit in traps and do nothing.

That was our definition of fun then. Now, I'm grown. I've grown, and I'm tired. That meant if this relationship was going to stand a chance, if you really wanted to prove to me you were serious about us being together, then you've got to grow the fuck up and get your shit together. You've got to *stop*! Make your mind up of what you want the most. I'm not playing *house* with no nigga who still wants to play in the neighborhood! That's not what I deserved.

I saw things in him that not only others couldn't, but that he couldn't even see in himself. I could see and see past that "mask" he wore that intimidated everybody else and scared them to stay on his good side. I saw that part of him that was family oriented, heart bigger than his chest, would give his last to you, spiritual and God fearing. For a minute I thought we were on the same page. He was one of the sweetest people I'd ever met, a gentleman. Wouldn't like me touching door handles, helped me around the house, cooked for me, gifts for no reason and he was very supportive of whatever it was I had going on.

The best Father a child could ask for. We moved as a unit. That was the guy that I was spoiled with since we met. It was easy for me to expect more because he'd shown me more for so long. He was playing himself short. The differences between us was causing so much conflict. He wasn't as happy as he used to be. For the first time, I was feeling the wrath right along with everybody else.

Not to mention I was heartbroken about my own things I was dealing with. Money was about the *only* thing I had that *wasn't* tearing me apart. Goes to show you that the better things get for you in life, the harder the enemy will work against you and will be the harder you'll have to fight. Peace and happiness are the things I was praying for.

Just imagine the same girl you grew up wanting to look like, act like and had looked up to your whole life, being the same woman years later that you had to go pick up from crack houses or visit in jail if you wanted to see her. A never-ending pain. When I was a little girl, I thought she was the most beautiful person and had some of the prettiest skin I had ever seen. I wanted a dark complexion just like her. Her thick, pretty hair. She was so fly in High School and smart as hell. My big sister. I love her so much man.

Sometimes too much. Having her anywhere near me turns into a sacrifice. She was always doing something. I have had my nephews Kae'lehn and Kae'meron, raising them, since the days they came home from the hospital. On and off we would send the kids to live with Tiffany, but it never worked out. The places she would have the boys and the people she'd have them around was crazy enough to make you want to really hurt her. Those boys are my world. Anything or anybody that hurts them, I hurt back. Even if that's their Mom or Dad. When Tiffany was five months pregnant with my niece Saniyah, she went into labor.

That was Christmas Eve, 2005. Christmas Day, Saniyah passed. I was heartbroken. Every pregnancy before my niece, my sister miscarried. It wasn't until these boys that I was given the opportunity to be an Aunt. They were like my kids. My sister gave birth, and since I was 15yrs old, they've been with me. I don't play not one game about them. I don't want them not to have a childhood the way I didn't from being in adult situations, so that's why I step in the way I do to try and protect them.

They deserve to be kids and do what every other normal kid is spending their days doing. They've seen things no child should have seen at only 10 and 11 years old. The stories they would tell me about would blow your mind. Everything from them being left at home alone all day with nothing to eat, being jumped on by teenage kids, to sitting in motels while their Mom was getting high in the bathroom with men dressed up as women or other people they don't even know. Never any structure, rules or consistency. At times, I've been so angry with my sister that I've *felt* like I hated her.

I hated her for manipulating our family – GiGi, my Mom. I hated her for lying, stealing, I hated her for loving heroin, crack and pills more than she loved us. More than she loved her kids. I had a guy say to me, *"Your sister is a hustler. That's one thing nobody can take from her. She's just hustling for the wrong reasons. She makes at least $10k a month or better and spends it all on this shit. If she was giving that to her kids and keeping it to herself, she would be doing real good right now."* But there has always been that sisterly love I have for her that no matter *how* much hate she made me *feel* towards her, the way I love her as my sister, overpowered every time.

This is a self-destructive habit that's gotten worse and worse over time. I think it started with the pills; Percocets. When the addiction builds, and the prices of pills get too expensive, you move on to what's cheaper, easiest to find and is still giving you the high you're chasing. I guess the rest of the stuff finds its own way once you sit and get froze with enough different people. She no longer cared about how she looked, every day was a party. Like she'd given up on herself and was living life by whatever means.

It's painful to watch someone you care about and love that much, down bad like that. Especially when you're used to seeing them up. Tiffany kept nice places and nice cars. She kept good jobs and was the one who'd promote through departments in weeks. How could she let the devil in and steal her from us like that? The boys. They're all I can think about.

This hurts them more than anything. It has really mentally fucked them up. They have suffered. There would be days my sister would get in my car, had been up for days and smelled so bad, I'd make her get back out and would take my nephews with me so I could spend time with them.

My hurt turned into anger and hate. I never thought I'd be down on my knees, begging God to please give me my sister back. I had already done this before when he took Taneisha to Heaven. This person wasn't who I knew. Every time I looked over and Tiffany was nodding off in front of her kids, them yelling at her to wake up, I literally had to fight the urge to keep my hands off her. How could you be so selfish?

Mom didn't do us like this! I don't know where she went wrong or what happened that pulled her into this, but it has been one of those things I mentioned that has torn me apart for years. So when I say both me and LA were going through it, we were! Bad. This is all the type of extra shit that was playing its own part in our relationship. Some way, everything *outside* of our relationship, got right in the middle of it and caused chaos.

In all of the four years of I've known LA, not ever did he once think of calling me anything other than who I was or the nicknames he had for me. Argument or not, we didn't disrespect each other. Not this day, and from then we only got worse. I started being every bitch in the book. Let me just say this; if a man will call you bitch once, he'll call you a million more and any man who'll call you a bitch will do anything. We overlook the word too often in my opinion. Him calling me out my name for the first time should have been a sign to me that he had lost all respect for our relationship. Know that your man does not, and couldn't possibly consider you his Queen if he can refer to you as bitch's. *Dumb ass bitch. Stupid bitch.* It's degrading. That's like calling me *nothing, w*orthless. He went from doing this in arguments, to in front of other people. All these are red flags and signs to get the fuck away, but I didn't.

Also know that when he stops respecting you, so does anyone connected to him. So never let things get as far as I did. Before you go ignoring shit, be clear on the fact that abuse is abuse. Besides the visible scars, there's no difference. Verbal turns physical fast. I kept making excuses to myself *why*. Why was I taking up for and giving "reasons" why he did it? Why was I trying to make myself believe that this was a phase and as soon as he could wrap his mind around what he was doing, he would stop? Me and LA would fight like mortal combat. All of this was happening in our home, so nobody really knew. Nobody but his Mom, because he told her everything. If she knew something, you didn't have to worry about it being repeated. Not even to her Husband. She would come to get her son, and he would take his stuff and leave. A couple days later, he'd be back. We were so toxic and couldn't stay away. It's surprising to know someone who's viewed to be so strong in the eyes of so many, was so weak when it came to walking away from the exact thing that was hurting me most.

One day, it happened in front of other people. Over Shanae and Rell's house. I remember calling LA's phone and not getting an answer for hours. We were supposed to be coming over their house for dinner, but when we got there, Rell hopped in with LA while I was in the kitchen talking to Shanae. He yelled into the house *Babe I'll be right back!* And the two of them sped off. I was so mad! Shanea was able to get a hold of Rell, and he said they were on their way back, they had to pick up Chasjuan.

These three fools pulled up, hunnie! Walked in, sat on the couch and kicked back like *nothing* had happened. I went outside, baby, the whole left side of my rental car was shot up! But shot up from the *inside!* I could tell from the holes, which way the bullets exited. I opened the car door, and there was a bloody coat and Halloween masks on the floor. There was splattered blood all on the doors and ceiling in the car. I couldn't believe it.

I ran back into the house, looked over into the kitchen and there was LA, standing over the sink eating. I blacked out. Snuffed him from the back! We fought all the way inside the bathroom. By this time I was screaming and crying. I can't remember who finally broke us up, but everybody was staring at us like *Wow. Is this what y'all do?* I just couldn't believe this nigga had gone out and got into a whole shootout in *my car* then had the audacity to grab hisself a bite to eat like shit was sweet.

Even though I was embarrassed by the things I was dealing with, I had convinced myself that all this mess is just what comes with love. Up and downs, and I needed to deal with and hold on. Ups and downs *are* part of any kind of relationship, but I'd be blowing smoke up your ass if I sat here and said what I went through was normal or ok. It wasn't. Hurt people, hurt people and to be honest, we were both hurt. I stayed, but I hadn't forgiven LA for anything he'd done. He was so damaged from his childhood and the way he grew up, the things he'd seen and the karma he was being dealt from the things he'd done to other people, that all those frustrations were taking over what we built, or thought we had.

We had a good history but the past year was crazy. It's sometimes better to take notice of what's going on in the *now*, because things change. People change. It was like no matter how hard we tried; he couldn't get right. There were days I wondered if God was allowing me to go through all this just to show me he didn't want me there. I thought I was being punished. So I started taking LaDarius with me to church. I thought that would help. We went every Sunday. Coincidently, damn near every sermon that Pastor Moore taught was about letting go of dead weight. He spoke about marriages, unhealthy relationships, I mean we sure did get what we were looking for, didn't we?

Everything I thought I stood for, I didn't. I don't know if we were obsessed with each other or what. This was like Bobby and Whitney minus the drugs. I knew I didn't want to leave him, so I just didn't talk about it, but I wanted out of this season of our lives. I did not want to give up on us; on him. I didn't want to give up on him and give him back to the people who had him before because I didn't trust anybody with his life but myself.

No female. No friend of his. I knew nobody would have his best interest like I would. Nobody would watch his back, have his back or protect his life how I would.

Nobody would tell him *this isn't smart to do* like I would. They just wanted to be around him because of a name and reputation. I didn't care about none of that. I felt like if something were to happen to him, it would be my fault because I could've just stayed. Eventually it would work out and save him. I would've never forgiven myself.

That's how I felt, not realizing that nobody can save someone who doesn't want to be. That was a job for him and God. I could play a part, but I couldn't do it alone. That's why I said at the beginning of this book, that I felt like my days with him were numbered. I really did. Only thing is I had no idea how much time I had left with him. But I did know in some way, *they were coming*. I had everything I wanted but peace. The material things started to feel like nothing. They actually are. They look good and feel good, but that's it.

They would have loved to had known about this side. What was going on at home remained in our home, while all the other drama and mess he had going everywhere else was being pulled right up on somebody's phone screen, being talked about in a group chat somewhere.

Chapter 11

LAST NAME: ALEXANDER

I was laying down in my bed. LA thought I was sleep. Our bedroom door was cracked and I overheard him and BJ saying something about a baby. LA was saying the baby looked like BJ, BJ was saying there was no way he could be the Dad because the dates weren't matching up. It was a back and forth debate. I could tell they were in there looking at a picture from what I was hearing.

So of course, I get up. I walked into the living room and told them to hand the phone over so I could see what they were in here talking about. Their eyes got big! They didn't know I was back there listening the whole time. I snatched the phone from LaDarius, and there was a picture pulled up in this girl's Facebook page. He was a newborn and didn't have many strong genetic features on him really.

I gave them back the phone and asked LA what the hell was going on. He told me a girl that he had messed with back before he went to prison, had just gotten a DNA test on her baby's father and he isn't the baby's Dad. He blew it off, told me I didn't have nothing to worry about because it happened when I was living in Atlanta, it wasn't his son, and he had only ever slept with the girl once. I didn't hear anything else about it.

Me being the Christian woman that I am, I remembered the girl's name from the picture that was pulled up. I want to say about two months later, I went back to her page and was mind blown by what I was looking at. This baby boy looked *identical* to LaDarius' Grandpa. I told him *Hunnie this little boy is a lot of things, not your son ain't one! Where is this girl at? Call her.* LA reached out, and we went over to her Mom's house to see the baby. He was gorgeous. The prettiest baby! He almost looked Indian, but looked *just like* LA! There wasn't no denying that!

After the first time he met his son, he never once denied him again. He knew like I did. I got in contact with the baby's Mom and told her I wanted her to get a DNA test too. Just so everything could be official, and LA could take care of his son the way he's supposed to. Even though we didn't have a doubt in our mind that Meir wasn't his. She had no desire to do it. I think she was more scared than anything, just personally didn't want to be a part of the drama LA came with. She I'm sure, was hearing about it and didn't want any parts. I didn't blame her! Everybody was so negative about the new baby.

Saying he didn't look like his other son, they wanted to know who the Mom was. Once they found out who she was, they automatically didn't like her. These people didn't even know her, and she damn sure hadn't done anything. They said she was lying; the baby isn't his. All of that. Who *would* want to be a part of that? During one of our talks, I finally got her to agree to get the test done. I really wanted to shut everybody up with facts. I fell in love with Mier the day I met him; I was on their side 100%! So now he would get both his sons and have them over to the house. They were both babies, a couple months apart, and I was pregnant.

Talk about doing the most! Daddy had his hands *full*! Me and Mier's Mom had a mutual respect for each other. The three of us had a relationship that you hardly EVER see, ANYWHERE. Never any beef or arguing. She gave us no type of problems whatsoever. If you were a stranger around us, it wouldn't have been clear who was the wife and who was the baby's mom, we just got along like that.

Neither of us had any reason to hate each other. Anytime he wanted to get his son; he could call and pull up. Sometimes he didn't even need to do all that. We'd pop up, LA would get him dressed and we left. There were times we would sit over her house for an hour or two, talking, eating dinner, chilling.

Her family was the same way with me when I came around. Like this little boy had the BEST co-parenting team a kid could ask for. Once LaDarius was gone away, I took initiative. I didn't want his son to suffer so I took it upon myself to do for him exactly what I knew his Dad would if he still had the opportunity to do so. Meir spent a lot of time with me and was spoiled!

Oh my God, I'd keep him dressed up so cute. A baby LA, literally. His Dad's side of the closet turned into his. I made room for him in my nephew's bedroom. They loved him! GiGi, my Mom, my sister, my homegirls, we all treated Mier like family. Never any STEPSON vibes. We were glad to have him around and just waiting on his baby sister.

Losing Hiyah

My entire pregnancy I had the luxury of no cravings, no pains, no sicknesses or complaints. I could still fit all my clothes. My Husband was very supportive. He didn't make me feel alone during my pregnancy, and his genuine excitement for his daughter was so sweet to watch.

We found out early on in my pregnancy that I was considered high-risk because of my blood pressure, but it never caused any complications through the trimesters. I didn't worry about it too much because *most* of the women in my family carry high-risk. My sister Tiffany miscarried several times and had one stillborn baby, who was also her daughter, before finally having her two boys and even then, Kae'meron was born prematurely.

His feet were transparent when she had him. Besides Tiffany, pretty much everyone else had overall healthy pregnancies and successful deliveries. My doctor otherwise, didn't give me any reason to believe I would have problems, he just kept a close eye on me. We were on a good track.

April 10, 2014. Los Angles, California. I had flown back home to be with my family because once LA was gone, my days got real boring. I was alone the majority of time, at home working. My cousins were all happy for me and couldn't wait to meet Hiyah. Auntie Michelle planned to throw me a baby shower out there, and I was going to stay until it was almost time to have her, then go back to Ohio. Normally in the mornings, I would get up to walk the beach, and I could always feel moving around in my belly. This morning, I want to say I walked for about 20-25 minutes and didn't feel anything the whole time. I also started feeling sick and real nauseated, so I went to my Mom's house and laid down. I ended up falling asleep for a couple hours. I woke up not feeling any movement. I was pushing my stomach all over, couldn't feel her budge. At this point, I was going into an anxiety attack and called 911.

The medics got there, started an IV and rushed me to the Hospital. Providence Little Company Of Mary Medical Center in Torrance. When we arrived at the hospital, I was taken straight into a room, then another room. Then another room. Some of my memories I have of that day are still too raw and way too personal to print on a piece of paper in a book, but I will say that it was a nightmare that I was having while wide awake. From beginning to end. I do remember the nurses hooking me up to the monitors, calling in a million different doctors and a Midwife.

Believe it or not, out of all the faces I saw come in, and out of my room, not many of them said anything to me at all. They spoke mostly amongst each other. Everybody was so rude. I don't know if it was because this is just how you're treated in situations like mine and they were uncomfortable or if it was because my Ohio insurance wasn't covering me in California.

I knew they were looking for Hiyah's heartbeat and was having a hard time finding it, but it wasn't until I heard one of them say to the other, "Yeah, there isn't one. We're going to start the gel doses" that I started screaming! *What did she say!? What's going on!?* I felt like I was getting ready to pass out from trying to catch my breath. Screaming! I didn't have control over none of it.

They were trying to get me to calm down so that I could hear what they were saying. *I'm sorry ma'am. Your baby has no heartbeat.* Something I would have never thought I would be told. Every word after that I couldn't hear, not even mumbling. I could see that they were talking to me, their mouths moving, but I couldn't hear a word they said.

The Midwife was explaining to me how everything was about to go, what I needed to do and what choices I had. It seemed to me like the energy of the nurses and doctors involved when you have to give birth to a stillborn is noticeably different, like less important than what you can hear from other rooms of Mothers with live babies. It's hard to imagine that, but it's true.

The strength God sent down while I was laying in that bed, for me to use was the *only* thing that kept me sane. I start dilating. My body was getting weak, but I wasn't really in any bad pain. Their first check on me I was at 4cm. Quick.

Everything was moving so fast. I could barely comprehend what was going on. All I could think about was I had to have our baby, and LaDarius would never get to meet her. The day she came was about the only positive life event he had to look forward to from where he was. He was obsessed with us and the idea of his own family. I was at peace with what I knew I was about to see. I was more worried about my Husband than I was myself. I knew I was going to be ok; it was her Dad.

I had her, but I didn't have her. God did. He'd taken her with him to Heaven.

Nasirra Ma'Hiyah Alexander. 4lbs, 14 ounces. 18 inches. She was perfect. His nose. My lips. Head full of jet black hair.

Ma'Hiyah had gotten a blood clot in her umbilical cord that cut off her oxygen and caused her to have a stroke. Our angel… thank you baby girl for giving me the experience of creating a life. I pray one day your brothers and sisters are as good to me as you were.

Chapter 12

THE INDICTMENT

In a matter of months, everything had changed; after only being home for seven months, Mario was in jail for murder. Tyke was on the run and LA had done a complete 360. He said after this, he was done with everything. I think reality was setting in for him and he was feeling that same *countdown* that gave me nightmares and anxiety at night.

We had been driving back and forth out of town with Tyk for a couple of weeks now. His face was all in the papers and posted up everywhere. They wanted him bad. He knew sooner or later this would run its course, but nobody was rushing it. Him and LA were trying to make what they could, while they could.

I remember being there with them mad as hell every night. I kept saying I wanted to go home. I didn't feel comfortable or safe where we were at. LA kept saying *Babe just please chill. I know you're tired. As soon as this is all gone, we're going home, and we're going to stay there.* I swear the whole time I was paranoid.

I could feel we were being followed. I just didn't want no surprises and the doors to be kicked in while I was in that house. I didn't even feel safe at night when we went to our room. Shit, they kick in hotel doors too. I was pregnant, restless and always waking up to every sound. I thought everything and everybody was the police.

All this was my reality, and at the same time, I still had to be a Leader. I still had an organization to run. I was sitting outside of the spot with my iPad, hosting webinars and conference calls. Teaching other women how to build their businesses and market products. The diversity! Only part I was missing when mentoring hundreds, was "...and by the way, stay away from the robbers, killers, and drug dealers."

Early in the afternoon, March 7th, 2014. Me and LA were finally on our way home to some peace and quite like he promised. Pulling into our neighborhood and down to where our apartment was, we saw a cruiser parked. It wasn't directly in front of where we lived but the fact that one was even there spooked Tyk.

There was *never* police out there unless somebody called them on *us* for fighting and arguing with each other. I asked Tyke, *you scared? - Hell yeah! Pull this muthafucka around just in case! Fuck that! I'm outta here!* I pulled the truck back around to the front of the complex and me, and LaDarius got out. LA said we would just walk to the back so that Tyk could hurry up and pull off.

We made it halfway through the complex, talking about getting in my car and going to get something to eat when a silver Ford stopped in front of us and a white man, jumped out. *Put your fucking hands up!!! Don't move! LA, put your hands up! You're under arrest!* My first thought was to run. *But you dumb ass, run where? They don't want you! What you want to run for? You ain't never ran from no cop. That's not even you. Just do what you've told your man to do when he comes in contact with the police - don't move, shut up.*

Under arrest for what!? - You have a warrant. That's for what! Eleven of them! Do not move! Keep your hands up! That cruiser we saw, pulled up. Arguing down these officers, telling them there's no way he could have a warrant, he had just been arrested and released less than a week ago. If he had a warrant, he wouldn't have been let go.

The detective in the silver card dug into his pocket and waived around this sheet of paper. *This is a secret indictment! They wouldn't have seen these warrants, but they're valid.* They didn't say anything else, handcuffed my Husband and put him in the back of the cruiser. Didn't read him his rights either.

Here I am now, looking dumb. Continuing my walk through the complex to our apartment by myself. Cold sweat and tears. The worst headache! I was heartbroken.

What now? I didn't even know what to do next or where to start. I couldn't help but to cry and laugh at the same time from looking over at the side of the couch to see all these white trash bags I had lined up against the wall before we left out of town. LA never got to them. It was his shit bagged up. I'd planned on putting him out when we got back, and he had no clue. I was done for good, for the hundredth time.

I did nothing but cry for about an hour. We had made it to the end of our pregnancy, and now I'm left alone to do all this on my own. Not only that, an eleven count indictment!? Wow. Guess this is it. I called Global Tel Link, added money to the phone and waited on him to dial my number. The next morning was his Arraignment. Bond was set at a cute, whopping, 1.2 Cuhzillion Dollars. No, it was a couple hundred thousand, and he sat there, for five months.

August 26, 2014, with the help of his Mom and a few friends, the bond was paid. I was up all night at Shanae and Rell's house, who lived not far from the jail, waiting for him to call and tell me to come on. I was so happy to have my man back home.

The hardest thing we'd ever had to go through together, we both had to do alone. Losing our daughter. I got apologies from him every day for not being able to be there. LA was determined for us to get pregnant again but it just wasn't happening. We knew with him fighting these cases from home that his time was limited, so he made every day count. I had enough sex with him to last me the rest of my life.

Mier's DNA test had come back 99.9%, but we were still waiting on one other person. She had been lying to him saying she already went but was really ducking and dodging the child support office's requests for testing for months. She didn't respond until LA came home and pressed the issue.

We must have called down to that office every other day asking her for an update. She told us that since all their attempts to reach the Mother had been unsuccessful, that they're going to be sending out a notice to her - that they would be terminating any type of government assistance she was receiving if she didn't comply within a certain time frame.

LA called her and told her what they told us and what would you know, the very next morning, she was on his line at 8, 9 am. I answered. *Yeah, Tell LA I'm on my way down there - good. He's on his way!* We got in the car and flew downtown. Five or six weeks later, the results were in.

After *all that* bullshit we went through with this girl, for almost two years and had almost cost him everything he had with me. Like I had always known in my heart... LaDarius was *not the Father*. As a matter fact, the test read 0.001%. The only thing they had in common was that they were both Males. But here's the sick part... Not only was he not the Father to her first son whom he was barely allowed to see because of me, she was confident enough to name her *newborn* after LaDarius too.

Stomach wasn't even *shaped* like it was my Husband's baby in there. *Neither* of those innocent babies she thought was funny to throw in my face and use against him as the center of this drama, was his. I was disgusted.

Babe, I ain't even gon' lie, I'm salty, but I feel like a weight was lifted off of me. This is sick! I don't ever want to go through no shit like that again. I really love that lil nigga man. She knew he wasn't my son the whole time. You did too! I gotta thank you for being the eyes in the back of my head and never letting up off what you believed even with everybody against you. This is why I'll always be for you no matter what. Because you're really for me and you don't tell me no wrong. Everything you've ever tried to get me to see or understand has only helped me. You make me better. I just want to move on with you and Mier and the family we will make together. I'm sorry I even put you through this.

Not that it's ok, but after seeing the way that *one* situation with this *one* broken girl almost turned LA's whole life upside down from all the dumb and devious things she did, *I see why* some guys just say fuck it. Like, my Mom was a single Mother of four, none of our Dad's helped her with nothing! Me and Taneisha really had it bad, she never heard from her Dad, and I don't even *know* mine! I know *of him*.

That's it. Dude missed my whole life. Not once has my Mom dogged her baby's fathers to us. She didn't fill our hearts with hate. She didn't program us to hate anybody. Not even our Fathers who left her to figure it out.

So when you have great Fathers like LaDarius, who actually *want to be there* and makes efforts to spend time with and support their children but can't because their bum ass Mom is in her feelings - is jealous of what him and another woman have so she takes it out through the relationship he has with his kids, it's like, ok cool! Be a single mother by choice.

A single woman doesn't mean you're a single Mom when you have a good man who's the Father of your child. Not everybody can understand that though. Nor do they realize how much more it hurts their own kids than it has the ability to hurt that man.

Then they will scream *I do this alone. My kids are good; we don't need no Daddy!* That's ignorant! *All kids need their Mother and their Father.* I damn sure needed mine, I just didn't have that choice. Charles Sparks ain't thinking about my ass! I turned out ok but why not want the *best* for your babies? If having the Dad around could possibly be worse for your kids than not having them around, because he's a bad person or whatever have you, that's different. But other than that, we've got to do better. Females like this make simple situations hard and guys who handle the situations the way he had handled it, make hard situations harder.

Especially for their girl to be in. It's a nuisance. Just like LA told me he would never go through that again, neither would I. With no man. You can't pay me to let anybody who's already suffering, to pull me into that space *with them*. It's a setup. I was only ever *a problem* because I told *the truth* and nobody wants to hear the truth because the truth hurts. It *really hurts* when the truth is about to change your life as you know it.

We were homeless for seven weeks while I was waiting for our unit to open up and become available. LA had moved me far up North, to be away from our surroundings. I didn't have to worry about running into anybody in New Albany. It was beautiful; I couldn't wait to get our keys! Everything was in storage.

We lived in hotel rooms, GiGi's and his sister's house while we waited. One night we ended up sleeping in the car. Long story. Just know I got my $24k worth out of it. The funny part is they thought we were staying the night because we wanted to. They didn't know we *had* to. We were literally getting dressed for church out the trunk of the car.

Indictment #2

October 13, 2014, LaDarius had been working while out on bond. This morning, before going to work at a new job he'd just got that morning, he was picking me up and taking me to breakfast. I remember being on FaceTime with him and him telling me to come outside. Before I could put my panties on, I heard panicking and crying. It was GiGi! *He hasn't done anything! What in the world is going on!?*

I heard a man's voice shout up the stairs, *Meagan, come down!* I threw my clothes on, got down the stairs, outside the door and LA was handcuffed. How did they know where we were? Nobody would've known to pick him up from my Grandma's house. We didn't even live here!

I wish I knew we were on the run. Another secret indictment. Tapped phones. Who knows who talking... here we go again. Sitting in the car with a look of disbelief in his eyes. *Call Mommy!* I can't believe this shit. He was only out seven weeks and already on his way back. I understood the first indictment once I saw the charges. I knew each day they were talking about because I was there. *This,* I had no idea. Complicity to murder? Who was killed? I had so many questions that I couldn't get answered. All I knew was, this is the end.

No bond.

What I Found Out: His eyewitness was his friend. LA hadn't even pulled the trigger. Not only that, he was never in the apartment when it happened. He had only tried to help the shooters. But this happened *three years ago*. When the boy needed his sentence lessened, he wrote a statement and swapped LA out.

All the charges against LaDarius were old. All except the guns. His past and the life he gave up had come back to take him away. He was so discouraged because since then he had made so many changes in the way he was living. Trying to be a family man now and it was too late. The prosecutors waited years to indict him in my opinion because they were waiting on one of two things... Him to be murdered or to murder someone else.

They were sitting back waiting for him to do enough bullshit to build up a case big enough against himself to where he was going to end up with no choice but to take a railroaded deal. Whatever they needed to make sure he was gone for good, they were willing to wait for. They do that to young black men. That's the way the game is structured. You lose, or you lose. This is also called being tricked off the streets. Your best bet is to stay out of these people's way, or they'll move you theirself.

...Sentenced to Eleven years and nine months in conclusion of an Alford plea, by Judge McIntosh. The closest thing I had to everything, was gone.

Is there anything, Mr. Alexander, that you would like to say to the court?

"Well, I would first like to say that I apologize. I apologize to my Wife, who is here now standing behind me and has been there for me for years. My son and my parents for putting them through this. I would secondly like to apologize to the courts, for even being here, having these cases heard. I should be home right now, handling my business. I'm 25. All I want to do at this point is take care of my family. My time away I'll use to become the man they deserve... that's all Sir."

The Judge replied, "I don't believe you're a bad person like a lot of the other young men I've tried over the years. I just honestly think you've been in the wrong places at the wrong times and you've been around the wrong people a time or two. I'll tell you what, if I can get six years and six months from you with no throwing dope over the walls, no serious write up's, I will never deny your Judicial. You can go home. I just want to see change and growth."

- *"Yes Sir."*

DEDICATION

This book is dedicated to my daughter, Ma'Hiyah Nasirra Alexander. Your Dad and I prayed for you and got exactly what we prayed for. Creating you was no mistake, and neither were the things God decided to do instead. I've found so much peace in all of this that whenever your name is used with malice, it literally holds no power, no weight and is a complete waste of time. Just imagine if you were here... a spoiled princess! We love you, watch over us.

My world, my sister - the beautiful, late, Taneisha Shanee' Pitchford. I know you're proud of me for holding our family down like this. I sure do miss hearing your voice and seeing your big smile every day. Your laugh. I know you'd be somewhere right now, yelling from a back room what you want cooked for lunch! You should see Jayla; she looks just like you. La'Darius' Mother, Mrs. Toya Alexander, who was completely selfless in everything she did for everybody.

You were the true definition of a blessing to yours. My heart, Kevin "Lil Kev" Hughlett, 22, who was murdered in a Wendy's parking lot with an AK-47 rifle, January 15, 2013. He was so full of life and filled my adolescent years with headaches, missions, and loud laughs. I miss you so much. My childhood best friends, KeAira Britt and Stephanie Bass. Life is crazy, isn't it? I never had to question if you two were for me.

You're more like my sisters. I still don't think either of you being gone has hit me yet. I'm *too* ok. My friend Kiona Jones who left me down here way too soon. Girl, lol. I love you! My guy Lennell "PhatCat" Walton who was murdered July 6, 2014, and to every other life that was tricked off the streets for trusting this lifestyle. Deante "Lil Tae" Hairston, Dashawn "Evil" Smith, they may have given you life sentences, but you're still my favorite people. I know the *real* you. I hope you get that appeal.

They're not *Bad Guys*. This is just how they were labeled...

EPILOGUE

I believe everything happens for a reason, whether it's one we understand or not. I've gone through so much adversity and survived that often, the way I deal with tragedy or hard times, confuses people. Especially the enemy. Then, you'd be surprised the ones you're inspiring. To whom much is given, much is required. I know this. I'm human; I'm affected by things obviously, I'm a Pisces. I'm emotional as hell, but I'm not easily broken, beat or stopped. I don't give up. I don't give in.

I taught myself as a child to accept those things I cannot change. If there's nothing you can do about it, there's just *nothing* you can do, no matter *what* you do, so you might as well find the best way there is for you to move forward from where you are. It is what it is! That's how I made it through my sister's death. You can be as mad as you want to be, tear things up, crash out, scream, it may seem like it helped a little, but it doesn't change *anything*.

The two people who LA trusted the most were the ones who broke into our house while I was in California losing my daughter. They stole everything in there. I didn't let that take a toll on me even while I naturally, was supposed to be grieving. I knew for sure they needed it more than I did. Only part that tore me up was my computer they stole. It had all the pictures in it I took of Taneisha at the funeral home when I went to view her after she was dressed. That's something I can't get back, my sister's memories.

My life is testimony after testimony. I know when God is putting something in my way and it gets hard that he's using me to help somebody else who may not be as strong as I am. I'm always going to be ok, and if he can use me to help the next person, I'm all for it. We're always willing to let everyone use us *but God*. Why is that? Friends, family, men, women. We'd let them use us for years. Just like with this book. I was scared to tell this story, but there was a *reason* for it. I sat on it for years. There's still things I *had* to not mention for the obvious reasons.

But I didn't know if I was *ready* to be this raw, uncut and transparent with my life. I didn't know if I was *ready* to be viewed for what has *really* went on in my outside of business, offline, personal life that I've always kept private to protect, prevent and not provoke. When I first began writing, all this wasn't the plan.

This wasn't the purpose. I was just writing to have something to look back at. I wasn't going to publicly talk about things that I hadn't made it all the way through yet. But I sat up one day and thought about how this is so many boys, men, girls, and women's *right now* - and how it *just might* be that sign for them to actually believe that they're not the only one; it's happened to the people who don't *look like* it's ever happened to, it's going to be ok, this is not the end, and it *does get better*.

I thought like, you know what, f*** it! I've shared small snippets of how I grew up via social media, speaking at transitional group homes for troubled girls, webinars with my team, conversations with the kids I've given back to and sent to Prom, and having real talk with the attendees who show up to my events - looked over and they were crying. Opened the notifications, the emails and inboxes and people who I've never met a day in my life, were telling me, *Thank you so much! I needed to hear this today. Thank you for motivating and inspiring me to keep going.*

All these types of things. I realized I had impact and influence. People are listening. They're paying attention too. This is way bigger than just *ME*. I haven't come close to doing *half* of what I will in my life and just by sharing what's real; *this* is the result? Yeah. I'm not worried about a trial or tribulation. I'm favored. I'm covered, and I'm ok! Let it happen.

I can deal with it. Even when it hurts, I can take it. There's somebody who's ready to give up right now because they feel like they *can't*. I'd rather be able to say *Baby this is what I did when that same thing happened to me or when I was going through that.* Purpose is given to everybody; you have to find yours.

You can't be worried about what people think and what they have to say, you'll never make it to where you dream of being and live how you deserve to be living. If I would've done that, I'd be somewhere stuck and boxed in. The first business I started, my Mom told me it wouldn't work. I made close to a hundred thousand dollars my first year, and that's no cap. I've never been to college; I barely made it through grade school.

Statistics show I should have failed in life a long time ago. But yet, here I am, years later leading hundreds of women in business, every day. The same girls who were making jokes about what I was doing because it wasn't what everybody else was doing are the exact same girls I can find right now in my inbox asking me to have lunch with them so they can "pick my brain." You have to believe in your *damn* self! Your confidence, integrity, and consistency are the *only* things that are going to take you to the next level. You're the only person who can stop you. F*** them!

In the more recent years of my life, I had to begin to start watching people and paying attention to their ways. Understanding WHY they wanted to be around me or look like they're close. You'll notice how a lot of people will start coming out of nowhere or coming *back* from nowhere when things get good with you and will have ulterior motives. Everybody is not your friend.

You never know why someone is doing something. Don't let *outsiders* in. One of the biggest and most annoying misconceptions about me is that I'm a *boujie b**** with a stuck-up attitude*.

Only someone who's never sat down with me a day in their life could honestly say that. People get to know me or have worked with me and built relationships steaming from that and fall in love with who I am! They see *this girl is nothing like that. She just likes nice shit and likes nice shit for other people. But she's real and has a big heart. She takes good care of her people and only wants the best for them when it's all said and done.*

I'm blessed to look like *nothing* I've been through.

Add the Interested in writing and/or publishing a book?
Visit www.a2zbookspublishing.net

www.ingramcontent.com/pod-product-compliance
Lightning Source LLC
Chambersburg PA
CBHW052159110526
44591CB00012B/2005